WALKING THE LINE

There is No Time for Hate

Other books by Judith Gwinn Adrian

Nancer the Dancer: Myositis and Me
(2020) HenschelHAUS.
Reader's Choice – five stars

Tera's Tale: Rebel on the River
(2019) HenschelHAUS .
Finalist, Eric Hoffer/Montaigne Medal

In Warm Blood: Prison & Privilege, Hurt & Heart
Written with DarRen Morris
(2015) HenschelHAUS.
Finalist, USA Book Awards: 2015
non-fiction Multi-cultural and True Crime categories

Because I Am Jackie Millar
written with Jackie Millar
(2007 & 2010) Golden The Press

WALKING THE LINE

There is No Time for Hate

JOSHUA WILLIAM CLAUER
WITH JUDITH GWINN ADRIAN

Henschel
HAUS
publishing, inc.
MILWAUKEE, WISCONSIN

HenschelHAUS Publishing, Inc.
Milwaukee, WI 53220
www.henschelHAUSbooks.com

HenschelHAUS books may be purchased for educational, business, or sales promotional use. For information, please email info@henschelHAUSbooks.com

ISBN: 978159598-878-2
E-ISBN: 978159598-879-9
LCCN: 2021950537

Cover photo: Coach Clauer and Mateo striking a pose for their set.

Printed in the United States of America.

I am no less a man because I fear. I am no less a man because of mental health struggles. I am no less a man because only I get to decide what it means for me to be a man.

– Shawn Henfling

https://goodmenproject.com/author/shawn-henfling/

To the men and women who mentored me throughout life, to my beautiful daughter, Joshlynn Ann Clauer, and the young men and women I've had the pleasure of working with in what is often a rough, tough world.

The Bears —-Joshua and one of his boys, painted by DarRen Morris.

TABLE OF CONTENTS

ACKNOWLEDGMENTS

I want to acknowledge all the people who have helped make me the man I am today through your love, your kindness, your scrapes, and your authenticity. You know who you are: Maw and Dad, Joshlynn, the coaches who let me be #88—the punter.

All the doctors and nurses who have helped me deal with my heart condition and the cancer.

All you young people: this book is written to you! And the so, so many dear friends who have joined me in this life journey.

Thanks too to Linda Ketcham for writing the Foreword, all my MUM and Dane County Human Services co-workers and clients.

And Judith Gwinn Adrian, my co-author; DarRen Morris, artist; and Kira Henschel (HenschelHAUS), my publisher.

Joshua William Clauer
Madison, February 2022

FOREWORD

By Linda Ketcham, Executive Director, Just Dane
formerly Madison Area Urban Ministry (MUM)
Madison, Wisconsin

Part autobiography and part social commentary, *Walking the Line: There is No Time for Hate* leads the reader not only into author Joshua Clauer's challenges as a child, a teenager, and a man, but through his work in the field of criminal justice. Clauer walks us on a journey through a broken criminal justice system, or perhaps, as he notes, a system doing exactly what it was built to do: dehumanize and marginalize.

Clauer's own life story is one of a child, youth, and young man with his own trials of poverty, medical challenges, unrealized dreams, and ADHD; issues that, like so many of the youth with whom he now works, made achieving his dreams seem out of reach. Ultimately, Clauer made the choice to use those experiences — those feelings of isolation, disappointment, and anger — to connect with justice-involved youth.

Walking the Line shines a spotlight on the persistent problems in our communities, problems created in part by the justice system. These problems include:

- The harsh treatment of our children (especially children of color in our schools),

- The racial and ethnic disparities related to arrest, conviction, and decisions about punishment, and

- The impact of poverty on our youth in a society that holds up material possessions and wealth as measures of human worth and value.

In highlighting these issues, Clauer describes the ripples of harm created by the system, harm to children, parents, grandparents, and the larger community.

Utilizing his own struggles and the lessons he learned through his love of and participation in the game of football, Clauer reminds us that we are relational beings. We seek a sense of belonging, whether through a football team, a family, or a gang. We gather for safety and control, which is community. For too many of our children and youth, gangs serve as their community. Clauer has spent his personal and professional life seeking to build relationships, including:

- Building a sense of community with the individuals we cage in our prisons,

- Building connections with the people returning home after incarceration, and

- Building bonds with the children, youth, and young adults who are involved in, or teetering on, the periphery of our juvenile justice system.

Throughout the pages of *Walking the Line*, Clauer's kindness, commitment to, and concern for our children shines through. He believes in the power of love. Clauer challenges us to look beyond the worst mistake someone has made to see the whole person and to understand the entirety of their life. He reminds us that the children in our juvenile justice system are people. They are someone's child, sibling, grandchild, and friend. Their lives have value, even if they can't see it and even if much of our society would prefer to deny it by focusing on punishment instead of healing.

Clauer recognizes and calls out what many of us would prefer to ignore. Mass incarceration of both adults and children is a kind of warfare, particularly against Black and Brown bodies. Clauer never forgot what it felt like to experience loss, to feel isolated, to be disappointed, to struggle in school, and to be scared. He draws on those memories and those feelings to reach out to our youth and to offer support, without judgment, in a system filled with judgement and condemnation.

Clauer gets it. *Hurt people hurt people.* He also understands that when people who have been hurt have the opportunity and the resources to heal, amazing things can happen.

He recognizes that gang response intervention work is non-stop trauma. The kids are at a crossroads and are victims of a vicious world that creates cycles of never-ending confusion, loss, heartache, and tears.

He is in the trenches of that war, reaching out across and sometimes breaking what we in the human services field are told should be our boundaries — those rules that inform us we shouldn't tell our "clients" we care about them. Instead, Clauer builds authentic relationships, sharing some of his own journey and struggles with youth, and willingly responding to someone in-crisis "after hours."

In the pages of *Walking the Line*, we are privileged to follow the evolution of a career. Clauer, a practitioner in the field, has learned that the people in our justice system have much to teach us and that we in the field have much to learn. In very personal terms, he builds a bridge for practitioners in the field between the academic evidence-based practices and the need to develop authentic relationships. He knows how to be in proximity with individuals caught up in the system, seeing them, valuing them, and being willing to redraw the boundaries to be able to help address the needs of the young people with whom he works.

Walking the Line reminds us that our work must be about more than addressing the wounds caused by institutionalized racism, poverty, and trauma. We have to reimagine our work and create new ways to build a community that is safe and equitable for everyone, including our youth.

Walking the Line is an affirmation for our youth that they are valuable and deserving of love. It's also a call to remember our humanity and a call to action for adults and practitioners.

MESSAGE TO MY READERS, ESPECIALLY THE YOUTH

I hope that all people and all ages can get something out of this book. However, I wrote this book for you, the youth.

I wrote it for several reasons that I hold deep in my heart. Several years ago, while working with a group of juvenile boys, I gave them each a journal so they could write about their daily lives. I was met with, *Why? Could I get rich?* A few laughs and then, *Not me!* Still, it went well for a few weeks but then everyone gave up. The journals were powerful, by the way, and they discussed everything from being poor to getting shaken down by the police.

My response was, *Why not you? Why can't you be a writer? Why can't you tell your story?* I even explained that I was a learning disability student, and was told, "You can't." I encouraged the boys in this group to teach the world that they can, to prove that they could do anything they set their minds to.

They did not write their stories.

Unfortunately, since that day—years ago now—one has been stabbed, one is in adult prison, one is on his way to adult prison, all joined a gang, all were incarcerated as juveniles, and two are running the streets looking over their shoulders.

I wrote this book for you all to see it can be done even if the world tells you that it can't. I wrote this book so that you can be understood and can be motivated to be great. I did this by opening up my life for you, my saddest days and the best days ever. I want to leave you on a positive note from the heart and I want you to realize that I am coming at you and keeping it 100.

***

Dear Youth,

Over the past 21 years, I have experienced so much with you all, you diverse populations of beautiful people. You have taught me so much about myself and my life. No college class could have taught me like you have. I have witnessed greatness in the making and have seen a few dreams come true. I have also witnessed great struggles that led to traumatic and tragic endings.

I have been saddened that our society doesn't listen to your cries for help. The game of life is real and you have all taught me to fight harder and when I say fight, I mean fight. Sometimes, we fight with our minds. We don't always have to use our fists, yell and scream in a violent rage.

The days of fist fights to settle anything are over and this might sound crazy, but that is sad to me. I mentored a young adult who died for being old-fashioned with fight. He whooped a dude, fair and square, and when he got a call to go squash the situation, he obliged. He went to the location to shake hands, move on from the beef, and call an end to fighting. But he was shot and killed when he got out of the car. While his body lay there dying, the shooter spit in his face and ran. The shooter was caught and sent to prison, but his choice created an earthquake that shattered hearts, minds, neighborhoods, children, and families. Because he was weak in the mind and never got help, he forever changed so many people because he couldn't take a loss of getting his ass whooped. Be a hell of a different scenario if he would have just shaken hands and called it a day.

I am so tired of funerals and hood shrines of dead young people. There is never any time for hate. Hate is a simple man's excuse for not liking himself. Hate is a lot like bullying: taking out your own anger on other people to make yourself feel good for a moment. Hate mixed with a little jealousy, fear, and envy will never create a winner.

I have known plenty of people who have gotten shot or killed over the most trivial s**t ever, like hating what someone had, did, how they looked, how they acted disrespectful, how much money they had, or the car they were driving.

Of course, I understand the neighborhood pressure around telling and don't do it if it puts you and your family in danger. However, there are some things that must be told. The street code doesn't exist, at least it's not followed as much as you think it is. Snitches get stiches and wind up in ditches.

There are a lot more snitches than code holders. I know a dude who planned a gas station robbery with a friend. Dude told everyone to hit the floor. His friend was supposed to go empty everyone's pockets, but instead, he lay on the floor like a victim, then turned state's evidence on his friend, who was sent to prison.

The Gang. Gangbanging. It's nothing more than a bunch of hurt people, hurting people. It is cutthroat, yawl, and don't forget that. When you are not heard and lack positivity around you, that gang looks pretty good. I get it. To be honest, a few concepts surrounding the creation of gangs are very interesting and highly important to life, but just not the criminal aspect that almost always happens. Just think of what you could do with a gang that does only positive things? But it wouldn't be called a gang then, would it? It would be called a business, a franchise, or a team.

So many of you want to be successful and mostly have chosen sports and rap music as your preferred path. I think that is great. You can do it.

However, I want to encourage you to do so with an open mindset. For your dream to be obtainable, you have to have plans. Plan A all the way to Plan Z. Develop a solid work ethic, a never-give-up attitude, and be okay with constructive criticism.

Give yourselves options and realize that we live in a big world. There are many things you can do with your life, even if you don't think so. Also realize that there is more to life than just sports and rap music, although I do realize that this is what we see and it is an option they give us to get out.

- When they tell you that you can't, prove them wrong. It's easier said than done but the end result will be rewarding.

- Surround yourself with positive people and you will begin to feel your growth. On the other hand, if you surround yourself with negative people, you will feel yourself sink into a hole that you might need a ladder to get out of, or it might just keep you down there.

- A prison-lifer once said that if he had to give youth advice, he would suggest starting by making a list of everyone you know. Then put a red mark by everyone you have done dirt with. Erase them off the page and out of your life.

- Don't be embarrassed of who you are because you are beautiful and realize no one wants to hear a story about someone making it who had everything given to them without struggle.

- The struggle is what makes us who we are and to be very honest, each of you are built for success because of it. If you can make it through the struggle I have witnessed you going through, you can do anything you want. You are warriors and that is who I would want on my team.

- Recognize when you are hurt mentally. Take care of it. Our brain is just as important as any other part of our anatomy and if it isn't healthy, we are not healthy. Too often we are lied to about mental strength and what that strength needs to look like.

- It is okay to ask for help. It's okay to cry. It's okay to seek confirmation that you are hurting, but it's never okay to ignore the hurt. If ignored, it is a recipe for failure. Believe me, I know what it feels like to hide.

I truly hope that each of you enjoys the book and gets something from it. I hope it inspires each of you to write your own book now. I put it all out there for you and believe me, it wasn't easy for me to do; I did that for you. It is important for me to keep it real and show my vulnerability if I am asking you to show me yours.

Each of you is a good kid with the world at your fingertips. If you want to be a football star, you have to work at it. It means going to school, following the rules, and setting goals. Set the bar high but make sure you have other plans along the way. Maybe you won't be a star football player but maybe you will be a star coach, game announcer, TV host, owner of a football production company, a sports agent, a sports photographer, trainer, team pastor, equipment manager, marketing director, ticket seller, a shoe designer, or a team owner.

The same goes with every goal you make in life. Dream big ...

Thank you for your time and I love y'all.

Sincerely,
Coach Clauer

PREFACE

FOOTBALL—FIRST CONVERSATIONS

I came into this world as the boy with a bad heart. All I wanted was to become my hero, Walter Payton, AKA "Sweetness." An only child, growing up in small-town Lancaster, Wisconsin, I discussed this dream with footballs — any football — because they were great listeners and trusted brothers. We discussed how I really did not like punters and kickers, but to be part of the team, I would do anything to the best of my ability. Oh, my God, just let me play football!

I am a man living with ADHD (attention-deficit/hyperactivity disorder), a momma's boy, and a devoted daddy to my daughter.

From prison guard to parole agent to nurturing returning prisoners, and now to gang intervention work, I am one of the fellas. On the best of days, these fellas call me Coach.

Football brings involvement and enthusiasm, positive identity, safety, pride, and wellness. It teaches cultural values, including hard work. It is our community connection. Our nexus. Go team!

***

Archaeologists constantly find clues from earlier human life. They spend years and careers studying geography, scanning the land for signs, and digging into history. But the one thing they cannot ever fully grasp is the essence. What was life truly like; what were these people thinking and feeling?

Reading my story, you are going to meet a boy who was, at times, lost. Some experiences make us; some try to break us. Everything has a role in building who we become.

You will read about how fortunate I was to have walked my path surrounded by loving people: my parents, my grandparents, and my coaches. They shaped me. They taught me that my eyes are cameras and that my brain is a filing cabinet.

My camera has been rolling for 48 years. My eyes have taken in some of the most magnificent settings life can offer and have also caught a lot of traumatic footage from war zones; footage that will not receive motion picture awards. On these pages, you will meet an athlete, a father, a coach, a mistake-maker, and your brother in this life.

One central insight for me is that there is *No Time for Hate*. A thousand years from now, I do not want anyone to dig up my part of the world and find that life possibly ended because of hate. I want them to uncover evidence of strong, intelligent people who could get past the most difficult challenges. Warriors.

I know that in today's world, we exist in different realms divided by huge lines scratched in the gravel. The lines differentiate the many inequalities that can be devastating for the economically poor and too often destructive for persons of diverse colors. We are walking the lines.

I have dedicated my life to promoting changes in our erratic systems, which are beasts that too often seek to eat everything and everyone in their paths. The only way to kill the beasts is to genuinely come together to affect change. I develop relationships with all people, regardless of their circumstances or where they fall in the mix of humanity. I love unconditionally. These relationships define everything about me, from the work I do to where I choose to live.

Each of us has a unique and valuable story. Some show up on the surface; some are tucked deep away. All hold value. There are prisons and graveyards full of buried stories that may never be heard, which is a loss to us all. Our stories are a fingerprint of our earthly existence. The world does want to know about us, to care about us, to never give up on us.

I am giving you, my readers, my most precious gifts. I am giving you my time and my story. You are going to meet a man who is still learning, but I offer my life experiences in hopes that one day they can help you make that big decision in your life, or get after that goal, or realize that you can overcome anything. And I can't wait to take pictures, with my eyes, of your successes.

My name is Joshua William Clauer. This is the story of my life, so far, on planet Earth. Thank all of you who have been a part of it. I wish I were writing this as a retired National Football League player, but I am not. I am writing this as a man. This is me. Love you.

REAL RECOGNIZE REAL, GAME RECOGNIZE GAME, AND LOVE RECOGNIZE HEART

If I had been born an inner-city kid, facing the challenges that I did, I wouldn't have made it.

If I had not been the only child in my parents' small, tight circle of post-Vietnam war friends who shepherded me, I wouldn't have made it.

If I had been a teen in a huge school where no one cared about me, I'd have gotten lost in those faceless classrooms and dropped out. Done deal.

If I hadn't been around a group of solid football coaches and players, I would have made extremely poor choices and gang life would have been appealing.

Guess that old me was kind of lucky despite our major family stresses. I was born with White privilege and had two parents, at least some of the time. Even so, our little family had traumas with my dad finally circling into the VA mental hospital; my mom struggling with having no money; us having to move all the time; and me, laboring in school and dealing with health issues.

I know that my heart condition is truly no comparison to skin color, but I have empathy because I too have faced *No*. Understanding that *No* is a powerful word and can often determine our opportunities, I was fortunate that my differences were hidden in my chest, within my heart.

To survive, I learned to see when something's coming at you real or when it's coming at you fake. You pick up on that quick.

I look at the young Black youth I work with now in my community and see that their struggles resemble what I grew up with; that old me. I also realize I'll never know their battles. Because they were born Black or Brown, their lives are probably amplified by ten from what I went through. I can't imagine having the feelings I had as a youth and then adding in systemic racism.

JOSHUA WILLIAM CLAUER—WHO AM I?

A few weeks ago, I was asked what it means to be a man. My first thought was, *This is a trivial question, easy.* But as the days went by, I realized it just might be one of the hardest questions I have ever been asked. What does it mean to be a father or a friend or a coach?

That's hard stuff.

You try not to be generic, like, "I was born a boy so therefore I was born a man."

But what shapes who each man is, or becomes? The men I grew up around were hard-working, construction-type people. I'm a big guy but that isn't what defines me. A lot of people would say, "You're a pussy, Clauer." You look like a guy who would break my neck but, at the same time, you just gave me your last dime so I could buy work boots for that job.

I think we've been taught the wrong way. I say a real man is a caring, tender, loving human being.

***

My name is Joshua William Clauer.

Joshua was not a popular name in 1973. My father was going to name me Jeremiah but then thought Joshua sounded better. My parents wanted me to be unique which is why I try not to be called Josh. I have studied my name biblically and found that Joshua was a leader, a warrior, and was respected by Muslims.

I include William for several reasons, the biggest being that I am honored to be named after my grandpaw, who faced tremendous adversity. I wanted my name to mean something for the sake of the people who came before me. Make them proud.

Another reason is because a younger distant cousin had my same name, except with the middle initial M. He was frequently in trouble and, at times, people confused us.

One evening, my Jeep was pulled over by the police. My mom was driving, and my daughter and I were sitting in the back. When I got out, the officer screamed at me. "Get back in the car."

Then he asked, "Are you Joshua Clauer, the football player?"

"Yes, that one!"

"Okay, cool."

Another time, I lost a correctional officer job because the captain believed I was writing letters to inmates. In fact, it was my cousin writing his friends and old cellmates.

I never met my cousin and had planned to reach out to him after his incarceration. I feel guilty now because that didn't happen before he took his life. He was a Beetown, Wisconsin, kid who, from my understanding, suffered from depression and addiction. He left behind some beautiful children he loved very much.

FOOTBALL—THE EARLIEST

Two or three years of age. That is how old I was in the earliest pictures of me with a football, helmet, and pads. What brought on this love at such an early age? My mom says it was probably just a boy being a boy, but I think it was deeper.

We have pictures of my mother as a football cheerleader and as homecoming queen in the parade, holding a football.

At my grandmaw's (Maw's mom) house, there were pictures of my uncles in their football uniforms. They even had cardboard statues of themselves from when they played. We were all proud to be a part of the sport.

And at family gatherings? We watched games together. Excitement and joy.

Football brought the family I love even closer together. Love of family. Love of connections. Love of the intricacies and subtleties of the game.

WHO DO YOU LOVE? FAMILY.

My parents both came from hardship. They knew there was no time for hate in life, only time for work. Survival. For everyone, this life is a giant struggle. It is a four-quarter football game. "No time for this trivial s**t." That comment will come right out of my mother's mouth yet today.

Dad, wearing fatigues cut off into shorts, was playing pinball in a bar. He was just back from the Vietnam War when my parents met. Maw invited him to go for a bike ride.

They hit it off. I was probably made in the back of a Volkswagen would be my guess. A Volkswagen Beetle, a bug. Just playin'. I was born breach. Maw said, "It was so bad, I didn't even want to look at you." I think she might have had postpartum depression, so my dad did a lot of my initial nurturing.

From a very young age, I knew my family was unique.

For a while, we lived in the old Triple R Ranch farmhouse (a Manitowoc facility for juvenile delinquents), where my parents were house parents. We also lived in a trailer, and in a rundown house, a home my uncle built, and a prefab home on my grandmaw's land.

My parents smoked marijuana and hung tight with a small circle of friends who shared their interests. You grow up faster being around adults all the time. I always felt older than other kids because I had been part of adult conversations and learned I could make people laugh. These people were very loving to me as a little boy. Being an only child, my parents were my best friends, and their friends were like parents or siblings to me.

I don't think Dad was a hippie, just a Vietnam vet who liked to get high. I knew a lot about the Vietnam War and the Ho Chi Minh Trail probably before I could tie my shoes. Dad has such love for the guys he served with in that war. He was a medic at NSA Da Nang. He experienced things that don't ever leave him.

These adults taught me values very early that became me: the importance of being part of a community, loving people for who they are, treating people like you want to be treated, not picking on others (this was so important because some of my cousins were unique with their special needs), and not judging.

7

Around other kids in school, I again understood my uniqueness. My interests were different because my house was filled with books pertaining to race, war, and Native Americans. Although I did not read them because reading wasn't really my thing, I looked at the photos, including the horrific 1972 image of Kim Phúc, burned and walking down a Vietnam road after a napalm gas attack. I remember grabbing that book and seeing her and thinking, *What the... ? She is naked.* Startling. When my dad talked about Vietnam, I connected his words with the pictures I saw in those books.

***

Dad was a poor kid from Beetown, Wisconsin, a place of poverty that was, in my eyes, much like Appalachia or the deep South. The town has a reputation for bars and fights.

Some people understand that coming from poverty brings a lot of similarities to racial difference. Growing up in the trailer park, the barrio, or on the reservation can give that same feeling of being less-than. It is never a good feeling. If you are White and complete some socially sanctioned goals, you can change and no longer be less-than. But if you carry color with you, it makes that struggle harder. I have a different understanding of these class and race lines than a lot of guys who look like me, and it is because of my parents.

Dad wasn't a big sports guy, but he did work out doing push-ups and curls. He had real big arm muscles. Older kids said, "Your dad's arms are huge." He hadn't played sports in school because it was too far to travel from Beetown, but as an adult he liked playing racquetball at a local court until the club rules changed and it became a private club. Dad didn't fit in. I remember hearing hurt around that.

Dad and I were opposites. We had conflicts. I often blamed myself for setting him off. Some clashes came because I was outgoing and wanted to put my dad in the limelight. I didn't understand why he avoided that light. Maybe if I did something big, I thought, I could get him to come out of his shell.

At my baseball games, people would ask, "Why doesn't your dad come to the games?" I'd point and reply, "He does. He is right up there." He would sit about a block away watching the games from a hillside, through binoculars. Later, we learned why.

Dad had longer hair and a big beard. He looked like a biker. One time, he had a job interview with guys who did not look like him. No babysitter was available during the interview time, so he took me with him. Needless to say, he did not get the damn job.

We were poor until Dad landed the job with the postal service that uplifted us, and he was making more than a living-wage. He built us a home near my grandmaw's house, on her land.

Next door, the neighbors were big into trapping and fishing to make a living. They kept their coonhounds in cars that sat on blocks in the yard. Their cigar-smoking children had built a boxing ring between those cars.

My parents bought me a pair of Sugar Ray Leonard boxing gloves to help me introduce myself. The kids asked if I wanted to fight and picked the guy who was nearest my age and size. He was excited to have a match-up for the day and pulled on his duct-taped gloves. He took all his frustrations out on me. I got rocked. These guys were big and over time, I think they helped me build up my speed.

But I learned to care a lot about these neighbors. To be included, I had to take part in what was happening. Hardship brings about a kind of toughness and they taught me even more about what it means to subsist on the edge.

Although Dad had finally obtained gainful employment, our home life continued going downhill. Better pay doesn't buy happiness. His job benefits saved us, financially, as his health spiraled down.

WHAT DOES IT MEAN TO "MAN UP"?

Dad had always been a quiet, shy man but he started to fall into reclusiveness and never wanted to leave the house. He didn't talk much. One day, he did not get out of bed and tried to drink a whole bottle of whiskey, as I remember. He was having debilitating wartime flashbacks, was irritable, and totally not himself. Safe to say he had seen some real messed up stuff in Vietnam. He saw people harmed and killed, like the photos in his books. He seen some disgusting racial stuff after Martin Luther King was shot in the U.S. It all damaged him a lot.

Dad was in the China Sea when King was killed. He was leisurely floating on his back, but the tide was taking him out farther and farther. A raft full of Black dudes came through and saved him; took him to shore. One of them said, "What the hell are we saving this honkey for?"

Dad said he just lay on the beach thinking, *Damn, thank you.*

As the war flashbacks intensified, Dad went to the Veteran's Hospital in Madison and then to Tomah, Wisconsin, where he was given powerful medications. He was in locked wards off and on for a year. It looked like punishment, like prison. I remember seeing another vet at the hospital constantly doing some weird gestures with his fingers, like he was squishing an invisible bug.

It all scared me.

After one hospital visit with my father, my mother asked if I had to use the bathroom before we left. I said, "No." But about five minutes later, I had to use the bathroom.

"Maw, I have to use the bathroom."

"I just asked you and you said no. Now you do? S**t your pants, then."

She wouldn't pull over. I ended up s**tting my pants. That was not my mother's normal behavior; it was totally out of character. I was so embarrassed and by the time we got home my underwear peeled off like Playdough.

My dad's PTSD wounded us all.

I started to be nervous all the time and think I had to use the bathroom in school, church, and everywhere we went. I'd leave rooms at the worst time, like in the middle of church or even getting off the stage during a school concert. I'd feel like I was going to pass out. My stomach was tight, like I was going to be sick. One time, I asked to use the bathroom at church.

I was told, "No, you sit here."

I said, "I gotta use the bathroom."

I got so worked up that when I finally did leave the service, rather than going to the bathroom, I just walked all the way home to get some fresh air and relief.

Watching Dad, I feared mental illness coming my way.

Now I was 12 and my dad was in that hospital. I guess I did not feel Maw and I had that protection from a man for the year Dad was gone. In my head, I had to man up and be Maw's protector, to defend her. Be the man. I sensed that we were afraid the well would run dry when it came to money.

I can remember doing things like taking a bath and measuring the bathwater just up to the first line of my finger, to save the expense. I can also remember getting soap in my penis one time and it was burning. Maw had to call my uncle to see, you know, what to do. It was awkward during puberty for sure, but those are the times that stick with you.

One day, there was a crime. I knew about it and saw some of it, but I did not tell anyone. I thought, *I want to tell on you, but I ain't got a man to back me up.* If I had told on something like that, I could guarantee I'd get my ass whupped by the offenders and it would be real bad. I didn't tell and I've lived with that guilt my entire life.

We did not have a man there, yet sometimes I realized it was better when he was gone because he was not the same dad I had started life with.

My mom had beautiful, long, red hair that hung well below her waistline. As a little boy, to go to sleep at night, I would have to touch her hair, maybe for security. It was cool and soothing.

It was the worst on weed-party nights because I would go to bed and her hair wouldn't be there so I would continuously ask her to come to my room. She would eventually give in, but I am sure I ruined many of their party nights.

When my dad got sick, I asked Maw, "What are we going to do?" She was so scared and irritable. It was just going to be the two of us during this time.

I imagine she flashed back to her childhood and the fears she faced. My grandpaw (Maw's dad) was a workhorse. He had a little farm and worked for the power company. He couldn't read or write but had an entrepreneurial mindset and a lot of respect in the community. But, at age 45, he died while working on the highlines.

Maw was one of seven kids. People went to the schools to pick up my mom and the others and bring them home. My grandmaw was screaming, "Do not believe what those men are saying." She couldn't imagine what had happened. Her husband was dead.

His death changed my mother's family forever. The poverty they had to endure is unimaginable to me.

So, my question of, "What are we going to do?" was far too real to her. On one ride home from the VA Hospital, she had a panic attack, sweating and breathing heavy. She thought it was a heart attack. She was all over the road and finally pulled over.

She turned to me and pleaded, "Can you drive us home?"

I was a kid. "I've never driven a car before. The road is dangerous. Just relax. Put the window down."

Finally, she drove, and we made it home.

While Dad was gone, one neighbor man tried to get friendly with Maw. "Just as friends," he said. I had a sense of hyper-alertness and didn't trust this guy. He kept coming over to try to watch a movie with us, or whatever.

One day, when Maw was at work, the local Chief of Police pulled up and told me, "Get back by your house." He had a squad car parked by the low-income duplex next door, where this guy lived. The chief yelled up to the window, "Turn that loud s**t off."

I was peeking around the corner. Suddenly, this too-friendly guy started throwing stuff at the chief. His stereo system. His TV.

It became clear that I was making the right choice in not wanting this guy around my mom. He was later arrested for pulling out a gun in a local restaurant.

I also remember playing outside one day and hiding from two of my classmates' mothers who were walking by. They did not see me. I heard one of them say, "Did you hear about him? He went crazy." They laughed.

What the f**k did that mean?

***

With my father being gone, my academics really went south. I struggled to get decent grades. Math was especially hard, and I couldn't read all that well. It was bad, but I did okay in history and politics because I could bring information about things like Vietnam into the classroom.

I loved everything about PE and the whole health field. I loved listening to health facts. And those teachers appreciated me. They saw an athlete. That was the class that, when I walked in the door, I felt at home. I thought, *I'm going to get an A in this class. And let everybody who can read and who does good in math, eat my dust on this track.* I had confidence in that class.

Still, school counselors started to pull me in to talk. I was feeling like I was dumb. My brain was shouting at me: Vietnam, crazy, worry, be the man.

When my dad got home, he was highly medicated. He was different. My parents argued. Dad left a couple of times and stayed with my grandparents, but he always came back. Still, there had been so much sadness.

FOOTBALL—YES, I TALK TO FOOTBALLS

Yes, it is true. I talk to footballs! Somewhat less so today, but still…

At some points in my life, restricted by my heart complications, I felt like I was stuck on an island or in the hole in a prison.

I began to imagine being in a different place: a place where dreams come true. In that place there was no threat of mental illness or death. In that place, I could truly be anything I wanted, even when something was trying to prevent me from getting there.

In this imaginary place, I met my good friend. No, more honestly, in this place I met my brother. The football!

My first real conversation with the football happened in my parents' backyard. Those talks were most crucial, and we developed trust relatively quickly, I think, because my football was a great listener. I began to trust that he would not say anything to anyone about our exchanges. I envisioned the ball as a messenger, a magician, a shapeshifter of sorts, and certainly my companion.

The football and I would talk about my struggles in academics, jams I'd get into, times my parents weren't getting along, and moments of happiness. We could cry or pray together when I felt hurt. But most importantly, we set goals and dreamed together.

My goals went from getting good grades, to staying in shape, to being humble, and to ultimately playing in the NFL where I would be able to give back to kids like me. I dreamed of going to hospitals throughout the country where there were sick children and spreading love and hope. I wanted to go to schools and talk to kids like me. My dreams were never selfish or materialistic (well, except for the added goal of someday buying my parents a big house with some land).

I know this sounds crazy, and maybe it is, but it worked for me.

MOMMA'S BOY

I'm a momma's boy. Maw is my baby. This means I trust her 100 percent, maybe even a little extra. My mother and I have been through everything together. Our bond is so strong, despite some battles. We are alike; both more outgoing.

Admittedly, she wasn't ever afraid to smack me, like that time I ran her new car over a fence and sort of forgot to mention it to her.

When I first started getting muscles, people would say, "Oh, you're getting big." I'd be grocery shopping with Maw, and she would tell them people, "I still ain't afraid to kick that ass." She made sure that because of her size, I wasn't getting over on her. Of all the people I've ever met in the world, and I don't care what prison I've been in, I'm most scared of Maw! Total respect.

She is a high-strung, full-of-life person — redhead, fair skin, freckles, and a fireball. At the same time, she is one of the funniest people I know, joking around probably 80 percent of the day.

She simply loves people. Loves them. She was a home health worker for elders for 30 years. She said it never felt like a job. She retired about 11 years ago so she could spend more time with my daughter, Joshlynn.

An elderly Jewish woman lived near our home. She had been in a concentration camp and was marked – a concentration camp tattoo. My mom would send me to her house to listen to her stories as she sat, rocking in that old creaky chair. Maw wanted me to understand people's life challenges and to see everyone as loveable, or at least engaging.

To this day, Maw starts conversations with homeless people. "How did you get into this situation?" Sometimes I worry about her because she is too generous and trusts everyone; she sees the world as it should be rather than as it (sometimes) is.

Near our home, there is a lady who sleeps in the woods and has all kinds of cats. She is schizophrenic or something. She dresses strange. Plain. So, my mom will sit out there by that woods, having conversations with this woman and probably thinking, *This woman could be Jesus, so I will give Jesus all my time right now*. (In my head, with my criminal justice background, I am thinking, *This could be a crazy-ass lady.*) But Maw says, "Remember that somebody, somewhere, loves every person just as I love you. Before you pick on them, before you punch them, before you have anything bad to say about them, remember they are loved." That's always been in my mind. This kind of awareness is one of Maw's gifts to me. She most definitely adores me. Imagine having this in your life, without reservation.

Once I started having my heart surgeries, Maw was always by my side making sure I was okay. Always. I had one surgery several years ago, as an adult, and Maw was there every single day.

***

Heart Dis-Ease. I was born with a heart murmur that may have been a result of my dad's Vietnam exposure to the herbicide Agent Orange, used by American troops to defoliate forests, expose enemy soldiers, and destroy crops. My uncle's child was born without a hand; it was high probability that too came from herbicide exposure. However, my family is also saturated with heart disease and defects. My family members wear our surgery scars like tattoos of a war we won, but hadn't asked to fight in.

I think I must have been around four and remember being in a dark room with dim lighting. My fever was so high. My family was giving me fluids and wiping me down with cold wet rags. Grandmaw said, "We need a doctor."

We learned I had an aortic valve stenosis, which is the shrinking of the heart valve causing a backflow of blood in the heart.

I've had to have regular checkups ever since and have known some of the University of Wisconsin Hospital staff from the beginnings to the ends of their careers.

Having this heart condition put a lot of stress and worry on my family and now that I am a father, I can't imagine what they went through. "What can he do? What can't he do? Will he die young?" My extended family was annoyingly protective of me. I was a kid who liked to run, jump, and play hard. Family members were always yelling at me, "Don't overdo it."

FOOTBALL—PLAN B

As early as grade school, I loved sports. I became obsessed with them, to be honest. Perhaps, it was because doctors were saying I'd never be able to participate.

My parents did let me play Little League baseball. I was pretty good and loved the outfield and hitting the s**t out of the ball. Caring coaches and passionate kids became my fraternity of friends. They picked an All-Star team from our league and I was chosen. This traveling team entered tournaments.

We were like the Bad News Bears, only good. Unlike some teams with full baseball attire, we showed up with all different colored T-shirts and blue jeans. This group of friends would play a major role in my life. I'm pretty sure I was known as the kid with the heart condition, but they still seemed to respect me for me.

I looked up to so many great athletes like Carl Lewis because of his speed and Michael Jordan because of his dunks. But I really loved Walter Payton of the Chicago Bears. His nickname was, and is, "Sweetness"! He was one of the only athletes I ever watched who made running a ball look like he was painting a beautiful picture, set to music. I remember wanting to watch every time he touched the ball because he might do something never seen before.

Around 6th or 7th grade, I asked my parents if I could do pushups with my heart condition. That may seem like a little thing to you, and looking back, even if they had said no, I still would have done them. I think by the 7th grade, I was doing about 500 a day, even at school. They made me feel good and I received the President's Fitness Award yearly. I was getting strong, quick, and was addicted to exercise and sports. I realize now I was burning off pain, stress, and traumas from my heart problems, my school problems, and my family challenges.

***

At the same time, everything around me felt like it was crumbling. All my friends were talking about flag football, track and field, and more. I couldn't wait to have my heart appointment before 7th grade to ask if I could play flag football.

I wrote down my questions and rehearsed how I was going to sell Dr. R on sports for me. It was a hard sell because he was from India. His Indian understudies told me that, in their country, people looked up to him like I looked up to Michael Jordan.

Dr R always smelled good, he had very clean tiny hands for precision work during surgery and he always wore beautiful gold Indian jewelry. You could smell his confidence. He wasn't afraid to say NO!

In case he said no, I had plotted different directions to come at the question. I had plans from A to Z.

I was always scared of those appointments because you never knew what your EKG (electrocardiogram) and echo (echocardiogram) would show. At that appointment, he listened to my heart and talked about a few concerns he wanted to monitor, but said I looked healthy. Knowing the routine, I knew I had to wait until the end of the appointment because my mom always said, "His time is important." I knew he would say, "Do you have any questions?" and before he could rush up and say, "It was nice to see you," I was ready. It was now time to advocate for myself.

"Dr. R, can I play organized sports?"

What was he writing in his chart?

He slowly looked up and said, "No, I do not want you to play organized sports. I want you to study so you don't have to do physical labor and harm your heart as an adult."

He couldn't understand why it meant that much to me. I moved on to Plan B, saying, "Can we compromise? If I can't play football, can I be the kicker and punter? In track, can I be the high jumper, long jumper, and 50-yard dash-man? And how about baseball? If you don't want me pushing myself, then these are areas where I would still be a part of the teams." I went on to explain each thing in detail. He listened in silence and finally said, "I will let you play those positions but nothing else."

I couldn't wait to get home to tell my friends! Even though I hated the limitations, I would take them. Well, another thing I must tell you is that I really did not like punters and kickers. But, if I had to do that to be a part of this team, I would do it to the best of my ability and dedicate all my time to it.

Oh, my God, let me do something! There was no way I was going to let them down: my teammates, my coaches, my family, or even myself. I made a promise to work my hardest, set goals, and never give up.

MY OWN TEE

School started. They announced the mandatory flag football meeting after school. The high school football coach gave a little speech and then introduced our middle school coaches. I was so excited to be in that room! I felt normal. At practice, we had our first mouth guards, a bag of footballs, and I had my own kicking tee.

We did high knees, butt kicks, jumping jacks, and as we stretched, the coach walked around talking to each of us. Man, I wished I could tell him I wanted to be his running back because I am quick and love that position. But I had to tell the truth. It was my first conversation with my first football coach.

Nervously, I said, "Coach, I am going to be your kicker and punter."

I remember the team got silent, like everyone knew something I didn't. Coach looked at me and said (and I knew everyone could hear), "Unfortunately, that doesn't happen until you are in high school, we don't NEED kickers and punters for what we are doing here."

Let me tell you, this was the first time I felt a crushing disappointment at that level. I had no idea life was made up of so many NOs. I was already going to have to be a pussy ass kicker or punter and you are telling me that you don't need me? And you are telling me this in front of my peers?

I was thinking, *Does this man know right now how bad that just hurt?*

He blew his whistle, and everyone else ran to the huddle. I slowly grabbed my tee and walked away across a big field, trying to make myself as tiny as I could be. Invisible. I got the f**k out of there before he could ask me to be the ball boy! That would have really f**ked me up!

I rode my bike home and remember that my eyes were so filled with tears it was like looking through a glass Coke bottle. When I walked in the door, I asked my parents to come inside because I had to tell them something. I started to cry and stutter. I stutter a lot when I get upset, worked up, scared, or nervous.

I said, "I give up." I told them what had happened. They embraced me and said, "Go outside and play smear with the boys right now. (It is a game when one guy has the ball, and everyone tries to tackle him.)

When I came back in, I felt a little better because I burnt some of it off. Maw and Dad said, "Start getting ready for track and practice kicking and punting."

My parents would have supported me for anything I could do, even if it were being the greatest harmonica player of all time. That backing of woke-parents helped.

***

Somehow, word traveled fast about my let-down. The guidance counselor, who was the previous football coach, brought me into his office. He was a very nice man and had a son in my class. They were a cowboy family; I really liked Mr. R. Rumor had it that the big scar on his face came from a bar fight.

He told me about playing college football at UW-River Falls, and I believe he got drafted into the NFL. He said things that day that may have changed my life forever, like the fact that he had once been a kicker. Then he said he knew the high school coach and would introduce me. Maybe I could attend a kicking or punting camp. He wanted me to work hard. He made sure I had a football and let me have the area from the goal post back to the playground for practice.

And then — those guys who used to lean up against the building during recess where I would have been if I hadn't been able to kick — those guys helped me by holding and retrieving the ball. And by being my friends. (Truly, thanks, guys, for that support and the enduring friendships!)

During that season, there was an NFL sponsored punt, pass, and kick competition. I practiced with an old, hard football that belonged to my mom's brother back in the day. The Friday before the competition, my mom brought home a can of florescent spray paint and put a stripe on the ball so I could practice the night before, in the dark.

The next day, it seemed like everyone showed up to the punt, pass, and kick. Here we go. If I was going to be their kicker someday, now was my time to shine.

I won the competition! To this day, I have that gold medal. That was the day I realized if I tried and put my mind to it, it could happen. It is kind of hard to explain because in the big picture of life a little punt, pass, and kick isn't much, unless you are a kid who thinks they've lost everything.

Things were looking up. I won the long jump at our track conference meet and set a personal goal of jumping 17 to 18 feet in hopes of being in the Junior Olympics and Badger State Games and got to attend a River Falls kicking camp where I excitedly met a Minnesota Vikings special teams coach and former a Vikings kicker.

In 8th grade, I worked out at a local man's private weight room until I got kicked out for stealing a *Penthouse* magazine and bringing it to school.

YOU CAN'T TELL BY LOOKING AT ME...
BALLOON VALVULOPLASTY

Suddenly, I started to get tired. Really tired. I would sleep in class (upsetting my teachers), go home, and sleep more. I remember hearing adults say, "Maybe he is just growing." I was also having a sharp ache or pain that was hard to describe. It ran down my wrist and arm.

One day in 8th grade art class, kids were playing a game of who could hold their breath the longest and turn red. I joined in and held my breath, but I passed out. When I got home, I told my parents, and they took me to UW Hospital, where an echocardiogram showed I had to undergo a valvuloplasty.

What's that?!

Balloon valvuloplasty is a procedure used to repair a narrowed heart valve. A catheter is inserted into your groin and when it reaches the stiff heart valve, a large balloon is inflated, pushing the valve open.

In addition to being upset by my need for this surgery, I was getting my first pubic hair. At age 14, I was becoming manly and was proud of that hair. But, no, they had to shave it off before the procedure. (Not another NO!) I was as bummed about that as I was about my heart trouble.

There were other kids in the hospital. One kid had hydrocephalus, which is fluid on the brain. His head was very enlarged, and it looked painful. A Beloit kid, across the hall, had a gunshot wound. And another kid got to keep golfer Greg Norman's trophy in his room during his treatments. There was one child who kept screaming. It wasn't the kind of crybaby bulls**t I had heard in school. That sound of pain was hard to hear.

The night before my heart procedure was one of the first times in my life I had been alone without an adult I loved near me. I couldn't ask my parents to stay with me, being manly. But I felt lonely, worried, and frankly outright scared. At the same time, I was glad I only had heart issues and not the kinds of things those other kids were facing, although the golf trophy was a nice touch.

That next morning my parents were standing in the hallway when the nurses took me to the operating room. I could see a look of love in my father's face but also sensed he knew he could not control what was happening, despite his Vietnam medical training.

The medications to relax me weren't doing the trick. I felt like I was being wheeled into a factory with bright lights overhead. People were talking to me nicely saying they were going to inject me with something to put me to sleep. Well, it still wasn't working. I felt a lot of pressure on my groin. There was a board that prevented me from seeing what they were doing but when I felt the dye flowing throughout my body, I sat up. My whole body was heating up from inside. I was afraid. I saw a stream of blood shoot up and said, "Blood!" The nurses kept saying, "That wasn't blood. Lie down, lie down." They were pushing on my shoulders and then I heard the doctor say, "Good night." The whole situation was extremely traumatic, and I do know what I saw.

A lot of parents talked to my classmates about what I was going through, and I got letters of support from them, but they didn't really understand. How could they?

My life changed. I already knew not playing sports was a challenge for me, but this added a whole new element.

When I got home from the surgery, I went with my team to a big track meet, although I was told I could only watch, not participate. I had just gotten the pressure bandage off that morning and was wearing street clothes.

At the meet, the track coach needed a few points to win the meet. He asked me if I could go out and do just one jump. I did the jump and we won.

Don't tell anyone.

Excerpts from Joshua's 8th grade journal about the balloon valvuloplasty

Keeping a journal helped me remember many of the stories in this book.

> April 12 -- I can't wait until tomorrow because I get out of school to go see the doctor in Madison. I always think it will be fun until I get there.

April 13 – I went to the doctor to see how my heart was doing. I took a echocardiogram. The echo said my valve was 65 percent closed. The doctor told me that I will have to have a balloon done soon and that I won't be able to play sports for the rest of the week. I am really scared to go to the hospital because the last time I went the pain was so bad I almost could have cried when they took pictures of my heart. I could feel the heat of the dye run through my body like a fireball burning out my insides. It is hard to explain how I feel inside but all I know is that it feels like I could cry for days. The reason I know its bad is because my dad even got tears in his eyes.

One of the hardest things to do will be to tell all my loved ones I am just scared that I am going to die. Can you imagine being 14 years of age and have to worry about death? I hope that after this operation I will be able to play sports because that has been my dream all of my life.

April 18 – I was in my hospital room for about a hour before anyone came to talk to me about my stay then all of a sudden tons of doctors started coming in and talked to me about what I was going to have done…When it was time for [my parents] to leave I went to the elevator and rode down with them and said goodbye. It was hard to say goodbye that night knowing that I wouldn't see them much the next day. So when they left I went to my room and lay there for hours wondering about what was going to happen during the operation. I know I can trust that doctor…

April 19 – My parents woke me up with their happy smiles telling me everything would be all right. I wanted to play my dad in ping-pong before I got ready to go in for my operation so we played. While we were playing I started to get bad pains in my arms and in my chest. The pains were different than any other pain I ever had before. These were the pains you always hope you never have. Then two doctors came in to put my IV in my arm. That didn't hurt at all. Since the IV was in my arm, I couldn't do anything but wait until they came in to get me to take me to the operating room. When they came to give me the shot to put me to sleep I was starting to get really scared and when they stuck it in my rump I got even worse. Then they brought in a stretcher and carried me down.

I can remember the looks on my parents faces when they took me away. I can remember looking at them and trying to smile to try to make them feel I wasn't scared any more, but I really was. When I got in the [operating] room, all the people seemed so serious. Then they gave me another shot that hurt like you couldn't believe. The doctor said he was going to put a dye in me. I know how this dye feels and I started telling him to stop. Then I started having a claustrophobia attack and went crazy but I couldn't do anything because I was strapped in tightly. When they woke me up the next time I was in my room. They found out that my valve was 85% blocked rather than 65% so it was worse than they thought. They had been able to reduce it to only 35% again. That made me and my family feel real good. My parents told me that I slept about 20 hours that day.

April 20 – Today when I woke up, my parents were already at the hospital. I am sure they are pretty sick of coming because it isn't a party seeing all of those sick kids. Today is the day I get to get out of this place. I am so sick of lying in bed. The doctor came to my room and talked to me. One of the most hardest things I will ever experience in my life I experienced right then. The doc told me that my athletic career was over for the rest of my life. Can you imagine being a athlete and not being able to do your thing. When that doctor told me that I lost a great deal of me…On the way home, I thought a lot about letting down the team but my parents said I could high jump and punt and kick.

April 25 – Today is my first full day of school that I have had in a long time. At the end of the day I started to feel kind of tired, but I was all right. I don't think some other kids really realize how important their health is.

FOOTBALL—WALTER PAYTON

My football and I were in a serious relationship. We went many places together.

As I concentrated on fundamentals and got to kick better, I wanted my footballs to be real. Real pigskin, I mean. I didn't want a cheap ball in my hands, made of plastic or some fake-ass rubber or something. There are some balls I just throw away; won't even use because somebody mistreated that ball or left it out in the rain.

When you first get a ball, it smells like a new leather coat. That is good, but a ball that has been worked smells even better. Have you ever smelled the grass stain on your jeans? Just like that. Leather and grass odors on a ball that has been worked. And I don't want to feel the roughness on a new ball where it has been sewn and the stitching sticks out a little.

Texture is important. I like to know that the bladder inside is broken down a little bit and it's got a little plumpness to it where you can really kill it. A lot of people don't realize that before a guy kicks off at the start of a game, he bends down and pushes on the ball a couple of times. He is heating the atoms inside the ball so they are active and will give it a better blow when he kicks it. And inflation should be pretty much to the max, well, just a little bit under max. Deflated won't go anywhere (but is easier to catch).

As I got older, I had multiple footballs, so I had multiple friends on the field, you know.

I punted the football in the backyard, in the hayfield, in the valley by the old folks' homes, at school, on the baseball diamond, in parking lots, on the beach, and even once in an alligator-infested Florida bayou. I punted him over roads, power lines, buildings, trees, creeks, and houses. Together, my football and I punted everywhere!

During those times, I would tell my football things like, "You can't go home until you hit five good spirals going 'this' distance. If you mess up, we must start over again." I would negotiate with the ball saying, "If I kick a spiral right now, and hit it over the top of this high line, my life is going to change." If I did it, Oh my God, it was real to me. Then I would just go home because I won for that day.

Once I got to high school and had football practice, my football and I spent hours together. While everybody else practiced plays, I didn't just stand around. For those three hours, I walked back and forth and back and forth and back and forth picking up the ball. If anybody thinks that, while the others were having fun over there practicing, I wasn't talking to that ball, they are crazy. The ball was my teammate. There is no way of knowing this for sure, but I am willing to bet that I have punted more footballs and walked more miles retrieving them than any other human being on the face of this earth.

As a kid, I had to settle for whatever kind of football I could get or afford. My grandmaw once gave me a football autographed by Walter Payton. I wasn't even going to play with that ball because she said, "Don't play with that ball! Don't take it nowhere. It's a keepsake and maybe someday it will be worth something."

And what a dumbass! I took it to school. Sneaked it. So proud to show it off on the playground.

It didn't come home. Somebody took the damned football.

***

I was fortunate that guys like Walter Payton were just down the street from me. You don't believe me? Eighteen summers of the Chicago Bears' Training Camp at the University of Wisconsin–Platteville (1984–2001). Sixteen miles via Wisconsin Highway 81. Pretty cool thing. Their coach wanted to get the Chicago Bears team away from their home atmosphere, so set up the rural Wisconsin camp in the hot isolation of a small college town, in August.

Walter Payton was so kind to me. I'd bug him for his wrist bands, and he'd tell me that if I was still around after practice, that band was mine. I remember looking at him and saying, "I'm going to be like you someday." He'd smile and rub my head. I was just thinking, *Wow, this man. He draws such a crowd, but he is so kind and so gentle.* He didn't even have to say anything to me. It was just his persona. Not only did this guy glide smoothly around the football field, when he walked to practice, he glided around other human beings. He was just like a dream.

Maybe he was a dream because of how his life ended. There he was, this great human being and his life ends, just like that with everyone in the world watching him dying.

Payton said, "Am I scared? Hell, yeah, I'm scared. Wouldn't you be scared? But it's not in my hands anymore. It's in God's hands." That may have been one of my first realizations about death. Any of us can get sick with anything on any given day."

Walter Payton's spirit meant so much to me that, even as an adult when I had my open-heart surgery, I wore an authentic Walter Payton football jersey that morning. I'm like "Sweetness," Payton's nickname. I needed to quit thinking negatively and start thinking positively. I had to have him back in my mind that day. I was scared. Would I survive the surgery? I don't think anybody could have truly understood why I wore that jersey to the hospital, but I did. I knew it would bring me back to an emotional time in my childhood when I had needed that, and as an adult I needed it again. I knew I needed to start thinking like an athlete; I needed those positive spirits (but couldn't really have taken my football to the hospital).

COACH, CAN WE TALK?

When my mentors, Mr. R and Coach H, introduced me to the football in 7th or 8th grade, they gave me hope and opportunity. They saw how my heart situation broke me. They knew the stuff that was going on with my dad. They understood that helping a young man at his tipping point is critical. Without help, a boy could go south, real fast.

Those men saved me from a lot of things. They saved my life. I don't know how far it could have gone, but they might even have saved me from suicide. I've never been the kind of guy to go down that deep, dark road but I think that that's where it happens for some. Like, "Man, I can't do nothing; there is nothing I can do."

Coach H was my main mentor throughout my football days. The last time I tried out at Camp Randall Stadium, he spackled [taped up] my feet for me before I drove to Madison.

In the gang prevention work I do today, I see kids just like I was—at that tipping point. There is a particular group of kids who live in certain neighborhoods and need mentoring. They don't play football because they have zero advocates or advocacy. Those who do play walk to and from practice, even if it is a long ways away.

Some of the coaches will never understand these kids' environments. The young people come to practice tired and hungry because maybe they have been up all night and they haven't eaten. The biggest thing they should have on a football field, in any poor location in this country, is a meal, or at least a jar of peanut butter. Make sure there are apples and oranges and stuff for them to eat. A lot of coaches do the best they can, but some sort of nutrition must be there.

Many people who do what I do for a job—helping kids avoid gang involvement—would never live in the neighborhoods where they work. For me, I want the local boys to see me, and you'd be surprised at how many times my doorbell rings.

"Can we talk?"

They need help just like I did. They may want to get into college. They may want to settle scores or talk to me about the relationship with their parents. And these conversations have been deep.

I've had young men show up who are so angry and hostile that I've told them, "Man, you need to sit down." I know I'm probably not supposed to do something like that with my job, with my career. But that's who I am as a man. I realize that there are rules and regulations around what I do 9 to 5, but when it comes to humanity, I'm not going to turn a kid away from my home because I'm not at work right now.

You are my neighbor. You are my friend. You are a young man I've come to love and enjoy.

"What's going on?"

"What's going on with you today?"

I'll tell you what, when a kid walks past my house and I can tell that he is having a bad day, I will talk to him. If it's a Saturday and he smells like weed, I'm not going to say anything about that. The most trivial freaking thing I could possibly say to him at that point in time is, "Man, you smell like weed. Let's talk about the weed first."

No, we need to talk about what's going on in his life right now and maybe the weed is going to help him open up and tell me a little more. I know weed saved my father; self-medicating kept him calm and cool. It may be the only thing that some kids have to grab ahold of.

FOOTBALL—WHAT IS YOUR HOPE, YOUR DREAM?

In 1992, I graduated from Lancaster Senior High School, probably toward the bottom of my class. I had talked to many colleges about football, baseball, and track after hearing people could get passed through to a college degree with athletic skills. My ACT scores—none of the three times I took that test—suggested I was college material.

Loras College, in Dubuque, Iowa, sent me some football letters and even a birthday card. I also talked with George Christ at UW–Platteville and told him I had gotten a 21 on the ACT, which would have put me in the top 57th percentile nationally. Not true, but how was I going to tell them that I was too stupid to come to their college?

I knew that going to college had the potential of disaster written all over it for me, so I tossed the military around in my head. Army, Navy, Air Force, and Marines' recruiters, one after another, found out about my heart condition. "Sorry."

I drove to Dubuque, Iowa, for an overnight recruitment visit at Loras College and was greeted by two big linemen. I could not believe the number of hot women who were clearly into football players. We partied, and I got so drunk I ended up puking with some big dude I didn't know who was sitting above me saying gross stuff to make me puke more. He was talking about licking an ashtray and eating a sun-soaked egg sandwich. When everyone went to sleep, I drove home. What a night!

I couldn't wait to tell my buddies about my decision; I was going to go to Loras. My grandmaw got our priest to write a support letter. My parents and I talked with the coaching staff about my academic problems and we were told not to worry. "Athletes had to have tutors and study tables."

It was the summer of 1992 and Joshua William Clauer was going to college!

I trained athletically all summer, but it was almost laughable, to be honest. I was homesick before I even left and Loras was less than 30 miles away. I was missing everything, especially my parents, grandparents, and best friends. I recall crying the last night after we got the car packed for my move. I felt I was heading into a complete disaster and only hoped football could get me by.

***

Fall athletes from all over the country arrived early for training camp. Some of the Black players showed up in a big car; their team coach had picked them up from their Chicago neighborhoods. One kid was pushing 300 pounds. I was about 165 soaking wet, but fast and could jump out the gym.

We were assigned lockers, helmets, and pads. "Hydrate and get to bed early. Practice begins before sunrise." I'd never set an alarm clock before so didn't sleep much. Would it go off? No worries, the guys were loud in the morning. We all headed to breakfast: omelets, fruit, cereal, and even ice cream if we wanted. I couldn't believe it.

One of the Black players said, "I shouldn't even be at this school. I should be Division 1." I was thinking the same thing about myself but wasn't going to say it because I was lucky to be in any college. It seemed many of us were in the same academic boat.

In line for the standing broad jump, one Black dude said, "White men can't jump." I was thinking I was about to blow these dudes' minds and yes, I had lift off. About the same when we ran the 40-yard dash. Feeling good. I was feeling good.

At our first official lunch, I chose to sit with the Black freshman. We were ordered to hydrate, and watermelon was rolled out. I love good watermelon. A White boy said, "Well, we know which table they are taking the melons to." Someone made a few monkey sounds. It didn't dawn on me right away, but then the room rocked with back-and-forth explosive language. One of the Black athletes replied, "Tell them what would happen if they came to our neighborhood." It got heated. The coaching staff stepped in.

What was I witnessing for the first time in my life? I was hearing Dubuque (where Loras College is located) live up to its reputation as the whitest county in America. The mayor had been working to bring African-Americans in to live and work. This push was met with bricks through windows, Ku Klux Klan recruitment, cross burnings, racist marches, and even home-grown hate organizations on the news. Locals did not want minorities "taking their jobs."

Welcome to your new home.

WHEN I WAS YOUR F**KIN' AGE...

Things were not going well; I was not keeping up with my studies. Skipping classes. I was spending more time going home and hanging out. I dropped out of Loras College. My grades sucked.

I was working construction as a helper and not feeling good about myself or my future. I came into the house drunk a couple of nights in a row. One night, I saw this cigarette butt light as I walked in. My dad was waiting for me. We got into it.

Dad said, "You ain't gonna be comin' into my house like that no more."

I bucked up on him and basically told him to get off my ass, "Who the f**k are you to say this to me."

I was so cock-sure of myself. I felt I was the man of this house; after all, he had been gone.

My dad stood up and we went nose to nose. I knew not to hit him but the anger I had held for so long, about so many things, came out. I may have been drunk, but there was realness to my fury.

We ended up rolling around on the floor. I think he took a swing at me. I couldn't believe it.

I thought, I'm not going to fight my dad. I knew he was still tough, and he could have f**ked me up. When he realized I had turned— become a man—he armed himself with a rolling pin. I mean, I was strong. Either way, in his mind, he was determined to win that fight.

My mom got on the phone and said, "I'm calling the police." She feared what the f**k was gonna happen.

Instead of the police, she called my grandpaw, who came over and saw the rolling pin. I didn't know my grandpaw would stick up for me, but he looked at that kitchen utensil, then at my dad, and demanded, "What the hell is this for? Put the son-of-a-bitch away. You go to bed."

During that fight, Dad said something that sticks with me to this day. He said, "When I was your f**kin' age, I was watching people f**kin' die."

I remember thinking that two worlds just met right there. So much friction.

I was sick of hearing about f**kin' Vietnam. I was sick again because as a boy, growing up, I should not have had to know so much bad s**t about that war. I just shouldn't have known all of that. I shouldn't have had to go to a VA Hospital and sit in a room and have a guy talk about how he f**kin' hated gooks and wanted to slit their throats, and there was a man and his wife, right by us. She was an Asian lady. That f**ked me up, upset me.

I was smart enough to know, even at that age, that this wasn't cool. That guy just said he don't like gooks. How should I even know what a gook was at my age? I knew, right when he said that, that it could bring trouble in this room. I mean, you just said you want to slit this guy's wife's throat! A whole room of husbands and wives, and I get dragged into this f**kin' thing. It is a so-called family council. I didn't want to hear that. None of it.

I wish Dad and I could have changed bodies. I think, with my mentality, I could have been able to survive more; we are different that way. I don't know how it might have messed me up later; it could have done the same thing, but I always feel really bad for him because that military stuff took the rest of his life from him. He could have been a successful engineer, but this smart guy volunteered to go to war. Then he comes back and goes to college and now his brain is so f**ked-up, he can't even sit in a classroom.

Dad has always been the one to say, "Don't get your hopes up."

HOW DO YOU DEAL WITH EMOTIONS? DEATH?

Grandmaw knew I dropped out of Loras.

I had a job as a mason tender, an assistant to a stone mason. Hard physical work. Work I should not have been doing with my heart condition. Work the doctors had told me to avoid. "Get an education," they told me. They might have added, "So you aren't carrying heavy s**t for eight to ten hours a day and wearing out your heart and increasing your chances of dying too early."

During that time, I was going to the bar probably every night, drinking a lot. I wasn't seeing anything good in my future and felt all my dreams for football and college had gone into the dumps. I blamed myself, "You should have known you could never reach those dreams." I felt dumb. I welcomed fights. Hit someone. Hit something. I wanted to get rid of my anger and my sadness.

At the same time, I knew this wasn't me. I had been raised to love all people. Have compassion. I knew I wasn't dumb. Something was wrong. Something had to click but I just didn't know what it was.

One day, I was working with a bricklayer who repeatedly called me the N word even though I was doing everything I could to help him. The other bricklayer could see I had enough of it. "Stop f**kin' callin' him that. We are all out here working our asses off in the hot sun; just shut the f**k up so we can get home. He is gettin' pissed off."

I thought, "If he calls me that word one more time, I'm going to take this shovel up against the side of his head." (There are situations that do bring a person to rage.)

I can't tell a Black man that I know how he feels because I'm not Black; I haven't lived 400 years of that history. But I'll tell you what. Even as a White guy being demeaned and called that derogatory name made me want to f**k him up.

It was my mother's oft repeated words — "Hate is so trivial, and we got all this work to get done" — that backed me off. She would say, "We're all the same; we're just trying to make it in this life."

Doing this extreme physical work, I tore the muscle off my shoulder bone. Every time I moved, I vomited from the pain. I called my grandmaw from a pay phone. She said, "You just turn that truck around and come home. Now."

I needed that kind of supportive authority message in that moment. In my family, you work. Period. Regardless. If your arm fell off, you still go to work. You can't just say you have a cold or don't feel good and not go to work. But my grandmaw had the power to get me to quit that day. The doctor gave me cortisone shots and said I should have surgery, but the company did not want to pay any medical bills. (I never got the shoulder surgery, and it still hurts to this day.)

***

Grandmaw was fearful for me. Afraid I would get in trouble if I continued in the construction trade; that it would take me off my square. She talked with me about doing something better with my life. "Be someone great." She leaned over the arm of her wheelchair and patted my face and told me, "Everything will be alright."

I told her, "I need you. I am afraid I won't be able to handle it if you die; afraid I'll go off the deep end." I begged her to dance with me to Garth Brooks' song, "The Dance," but she said, "We will do that on another day." I did not realize she meant we would dance in heaven.

And I'm glad I didn't know the way it all would end; the way it all would go.

That next week, my father called the owner of the brick company who came to the job site and told me to come down off the scaffolding. "Your father just called, and I have some bad news. Your dad said you are going to take this really hard. Your grandmother passed this morning. He wants you to come home."

I felt like my world ended.

I stopped to pick up my cousin on the way home. He was heartbroken, destroying his room, throwing stuff and that. I told him, "Cool down."

When we got to my parents' house, the whole family was there. Having everyone around made it a little easier. I don't know how people deal with losing somebody when they are alone without other people to be able to talk with and hold. That scares me.

Maw had been with my grandmaw when she died. She asked her, "Do you feel you can die today?" My grandmaw said, "Yeah." But she wanted to know where I was. My mom said, "It is okay to die. Just relax and go ahead. Go with it." They had left her body in bed so I

38

could see her. My mom and dad took me into her bedroom. I touched Grandmaw. I actually wanted to lie down next to her. I kissed her on her forehead. I held her hand and said a prayer.

It was the toughest day.

***

I don't know what would have happened if my college re-acceptance letter hadn't come shortly after Grandmaw's death. I took the letter as a sign. Grandmaw had talked with God. I loved her so much and I trusted her so completely that everything I did after her death I tried to do with her in mind. Everything from cleaning my skin to having sex, I felt she was watching. It was hard to do anything I thought she would disapprove of.

If I hadn't gone back to college or if I had failed again, I would have become a full-fledged alcoholic with four or five DUIs, disorderly conduct, and battery. No question.

There were four different college experiences where I worked to get my grades up before I finally graduated from Loras College in 1999. I know that Grandmaw's belief in me got me back on my square. She helped me finish what I had started.

When I returned to Loras, I was identified through the Lynch Learning Center as LD—having a learning disability. The Center provided additional support for students like me who have ADHD. People with Attention-Deficit/Hyperactivity Disorder are described as disorganized, lacking focus, and being forgetful. Bet you are smiling. I really am trying not to be disorganized in telling you my story. This was, and is, me. There was an entire center for students like me and staff who helped us.

At first, I did not tell other students where I was going when I headed for the Lynch Learning Center because I was a little ashamed. My LD teacher was kind, gentle, and pushed me to do my best with my learning disabilities. I felt loved and cared for. Together we did it and got my grades up. When I came to realize my learning style was just unique, I proudly walked through the Center doors with my hoodie off. I learned to accept the help I needed.

JOHN, BRO

The trigger for my learning disability diagnosis at Loras College came about because John died.

He shot himself. He was my cousin's best friend and another of my cousin's boyfriend. Because I was an only child, my cousins are my younger siblings. Very close.

It was a snowy day. John returned home from taking the snowblower to help a friend. There was a heated argument with his mom and stepfather (good people). The police were called, and John agreed to go with them but asked if he could first go back and grab his coat. In my mind, I can hear him saying, "I'll show you!" He retreated to his room, let out a big scream, and put the 20-caliber gun—hollow-point bullet—to his forehead. He shot himself between the eyes.

His split-second choice hurt so many people.

Did we luck out that John didn't take someone else's life besides his own that night? Could it have been mine? I sure would have intervened if I had been there. A lot of us would have.

The University of Wisconsin Hospital medivac helicopter couldn't fly safely, so the ambulance had to plow through the 70 miles to Madison.

In the subsequent days, I remember hearing things like, "His eyes are responding to light," then "His eyes are not responding to light." It was a situation that you knew wasn't going to have a good ending and his parents had to make that choice.

I am still haunted by how artificial the skin on his forehead looked as he lay in his casket.

***

A tiny-statured kid, John was extremely handsome with his combed-back black hair, beautiful dark eyes, olive skin, and a smile that set him apart from the rest. He was quirky and spunky. Also, he would never back down from anyone, anytime.

The summer before his death, I broke up a fight between him and a dude. I grabbed John and placed him on top of a car. When doing so, I felt something hard in his hand. He was doing a lot of s**t-talking and I remember wondering why he wasn't backing down from a fight he wouldn't win.

Brass knuckles. That was where his confidence was coming from.

He looked up to me; admired me, and always acknowledged that love when we were together. I was into working out and was feeling strong and looking good. He told me he wished he could put on muscle like I did. We were both into motorcycles, which was equivalent of alcohol for us. We weren't riding for satisfaction. Speed. It takes a special kind of guy who has that zero-to-100 mentality. He's sitting on a rocket ship that doesn't leave the ground. John's motorcycle was way too big for him but gave him a feeling of control and power.

John had wanted to be an architect and would have been a great one. He was so smart and already doing creative architectural drawings. At what point in life would he (or any of us) have realized that power comes from the mind? How do I raise my children? What kind of brother am I? What kind of man do I aspire to be?

Guilt came for me. A few days before his death, I made John hand over the gun when he was intent on confronting some guys who had disrespected him (and his girl). Later I gave the gun back. (Knowing what I do now, in my criminal justice work, I would never have done that.)

John's life and death put me at a crossroads where crucial life decisions were made about moving forward on the criminal justice track in college. Before that, my major, while struggling in school, was always around physical education because I was passionate about sports. John's death pushed me to realize that I wanted to help people. It furthered my thinking about the phrase, *hurt people hurt people*. We are all hurt in some form or fashion, but we handle this hurt differently.

My drinking was getting out of control, and I am not myself when I drink. I wasn't drinking to party, I realized; I was drinking to make myself feel better. I felt the sadness and depression behind my destructive behaviors. I would go out looking for a fight; I had an aggressive, competitive feeling. One time, friends dropped me off at home. Extremely drunk, I fell asleep in a snowbank. My mom came out and brought me in. She saved me.

I kept the brass knuckles I took from John that night and still have them. I also have one of his favorite T-shirts that I keep for encouragement.

When John died, it hurt my soul so bad that I looked for mental health help; that was when I got diagnosed with my ADHD learning disability at the Loras College Lynch Learning Center. That diagnosis helped me graduate from college.

John. Brother.
I hope you good up there. I am playing Boyz II Men as I write you. It's "Hard to Say Goodbye to Yesterday," to be exact. I will mix it up with a little Scarface and some Snoop and Dre. I remember how excited you were to play me the Doggystyle CD. Crazy how we could somehow relate to the music. The last time I saw you, I was putting you to bed on your mom's couch and trying to not wake anyone. We were so drunk. You said, "I love you," and you fell asleep. I hope you got that architect job you were applying for. I heard they pay good. I still have that purple-colored T-shirt that your mom gave me. I stopped by to talk to her right after you left for your final trip. You left your room a mess and tattooed the carpet with sadness.

I saw a picture of you that they put on a stone. It was that picture of you on the white and red hurricane racing bike. I said it then and I will say it now, *too much power between your legs*. I couldn't believe how fast you and Bobby were going when you drove past me mowing the cemetery. Y'all were a blur. I quit riding because I was getting too gutsy. Bobby and I outran a state boy on the way to Blackhawk Lake. Hid the bike and lay on the beach until we felt safe enough to get home. I think I hit 145 but was too scared to look down. Bobby was loving it but you know he from that life. I'm glad that part of my life is over with, to be honest.

Remember when you told me that you could talk to me about anything after we went and got that video that someone privately recorded. Still have to talk to you about that one. I remember that night you told me I should lift weights and be a body builder and that you thought I would make a good counselor. I took that to heart, bro.

After you left, I went to talk to a counselor and got put on Ritalin. Had one counselor at a place called DVR give me a test and the results said I should prepare to do fast food work. LOL. That means "laugh out loud" down here. One counselor hit it on the head. This Ritalin s**t has me reading pieces of books. I skipped all my classes one day and actually read the entire day. Never did that before. Switched my concentration to criminal justice. I wanted to help guys who think like us but do it differently by giving them that time.

Tried out for the NFL and had your favorite T-shirt under my shirt. Didn't make it but I am on to something now. Everyone was so beside themselves when you left. I was in communication with your brothers a lot, but lost contact. From what I hear, they are all doing good and your sister is now a big-time lawyer. I heard she was locking up high-profile gangsters for the Feds. Haven't seen your mom in years but I do see your dad from time to time. He proves over and over again that he has more energy than any man I have ever seen and surely is the best friend a lot of people could ever have.

We all wish you were still here. You sure did teach many of us about life, bro. I know you taught me. S**t, you saved my life. I am currently working with juvenile boys; most of them are Black. I love it. It doesn't even seem like a job. They are a lot like us. Young bulls, cock-strong, and know everything. I think of them as my own kids, man. They face even bigger challenges than I know you saw. I often talk about you to them: about choices and how those split-second decisions can change life on the now. Those decisions don't just change their lives but the lives of everyone around them and it never seems for the better. But I am on it.

Enough about me. Are you getting any ass up there? Or is it constant church services? Still riding that motorcycle? Do you stay in touch with your family? Man, you got to go to Jamaica if you haven't been yet. The Rasta Man surely has a gift. Where you're at, are there a lot of religions? I have learned something from many faiths, but I love that peace that the Rastafarian talking about. I also been getting in touch with some Native beliefs that make a lot of sense. The Muslims have a great message too, for men. How about you. What're you on now? Still a Catholic? Just curious.

I won't keep you. I am sure you are working on some job sight plans. Before I come see you, please make sure they have a gladiator type facility where the gladiators meet, football is cheap, and a place we can all hang out. Miss you and love you. —Clauer

DO YOU WANT TO BE SOMEBODY, OR NOT? SERIOUS-OFFENDER JUVENILE PAROLE OFFICER

I had switched my college major to criminal justice and was interning with the Dane County Narcotics Task Force gang unit, in Madison, Wisconsin, before my Loras College graduation.

My dad and his experiences really helped me.

That was 1998 and things have changed since then, so interns likely aren't allowed to be in an undercover car or involved in purchasing crack cocaine now. I did luck out because the cop I was working with had been one of my high school coaches and there was trust between us. He knew me.

When my college instructor came to see how my internship was going, I was wearing a bulletproof vest. He was like, "What the f**k. Joshua, you cannot do this. If you get killed during this internship, it is my ass."

I said, "No, I've got this."

He responded, "Well, you'd better write one hell of a good paper."

During the internship, a couple of things happened. I was there when a man walked across a parking lot and shot a guy. We were on Madison's South Side in a police car and the cop hit it. "Shots fired, shots fired." We were going at least 85, 90 miles an hour on the side of the packed Beltline highway. When I looked back, I could see nothing but cop cars coming from everywhere.

I'll never forget the stuff I saw in the parking lot that day. Somebody lost his life right there that day.

Crazy. The father of the boy who died showed up at the crime scene. He looked like he was from my hometown. Old country boy. They had told him his son had been in an accident. When he got to the site, the officer said his son had been shot. I remember the father's face.

I watched the life fade in this man's eyes. I couldn't believe it. This man's whole persona changed. I was like, "Holy f**k."

I was really shook.

The first person I called was my dad because he is who he is and had seen what he had seen. He was like, "Brother, this IS the world. This is our world. I protected you your whole life from this." He had. He did. I hadn't seen that. He was a protector.

My dad and I can connect now that I'm older; I can relate things I've seen to his experiences in Vietnam. I see him more as my people now. Even in our hard times, I've always given Dad kisses when we parted. He is my heart. He is my best friend. For real.

***

Working as a Serious Offender Juvenile Parole Officer was my first professional job. It was the year 2000. The job paid $11.45 an hour. I was surprised at that, but people told me, "Take the job because of the state benefits." They felt like I had hit a home run.

I was assigned to the northern-most part of Wisconsin — Rice Lake. My territory extended from Eau Claire to the Apostle Islands, about 150 miles.

I generally like working with gangbangers because, you know, it's gangbanging (being a member of a violent street gang). There were older guys who had raped or molested children; I told them, "Get out of my office. I cannot deal with you." I lose total respect; I am very biased that way and, as a professional, I need to know when I need to step away.

On a home visit to a Chicago gangbanger's home, his grandmother met me at the door. "He's not home." I hung out in town and when I went back, this large car pulled up full of big Black dudes who were obviously gangbanging and not in a good mood. They let the boy out of the car; he was so drunk or high he could barely walk.

There was no dialogue between us, but the angry looks these older guys gave me said, "Aw, we're f**ked. Here is this parole officer." I thought I was in trouble. But the boy's grandmother came out saying, "This is a good man who is just here to see if my boy's doing alright." I didn't want to make a stink about something minor like the drinking. I was in no position to do that so shook up with the older guys and told the young man, "Get it together."

There were and are some nature-based, arts, and mental health youth treatment centers up north. It may seem strange to send Black and Hispanic urban kids to the woods, but the idea is to expose them to a very different world. There are camping and excursion trips where they see bears and other wildlife. Some kids skyrocket their interest in the outdoors.

It can go the other way too. There was one group of three Black boys who stole a car. They were robbing cabins and looking for guns. They thought they were headed south, toward home, but they were driving north instead. They got arguing over a bag of candy – mixed flavors but they all wanted the same kind — and crashed the car. They ran.

It was Christmas trees that got them caught. One kid was wildly allergic to pine and they ran into a northern pine forest where he had a major reaction. They ended up in a remarkably small jail. Their first words to me were, "Get us outta here, man. You got to get us out of this jail. These people are crazy and racist. Take us back to Milwaukee."

I had some kids involved in serious crimes too. A female was with two older males. They pretended their car had broken down and went to the home of two elders who were helpfully welcoming. It was a set-up for robbery. They ended up killing the couple.

Another girl, Native American, was housed at the Southern Oaks Girl's School. She had poured scalding water on someone. I did a home visit on her reservation and then went to meet her. I liked her even though I had heard all these reports. "She is just an animal; hard to get along with." When we met in person, she said something that stuck with me. "I trust you because I know you are Indian." That blew my mind because I was the only one who knew that I could possibly have Indian blood in me.

We had a great conversation. She was very proud of being a Native girl.

She didn't participate in things the other girls were doing at the school until suddenly one morning, she offered to lead the exercise class. A tribal dance.

Then she went back to her cell, tied her sheets together, got on her knees, and leaned into the sheets. She killed herself.

We had to get her body back to the reservation fast for ceremonial reasons and I was adamant with the state that we need to do this now. That was a tough one.

If she had been out, I believe I could have been a mentor to her on the reservation. It bothers me that if we had been more culturally knowledgeable, it could have made a difference.

What might have happened if we had asked her why she did the dance that day? Other people who worked with her were very hurt by her death.

***

Part of my parole officer job was transporting kids from one location to another: always a driver with another officer in the back with the child. The kids were handcuffed.

We pulled into Southern Oaks Girls School with a White girl from Eau Claire. We put her in a holding cell with some big chicks from Milwaukee. One of the girls yelled, "Get in here, Glow Bug."

The girl looked at me like, "What! Do I have to stay here?"

One of the reasons I took her there was to shock the system. "Yes."

***

At Northwest Passage Residential Treatment Program, I had a little Mexican kid from South Milwaukee. I said to him, "So, you are a gang member?"

"No, I don't gangbang." He was looking for a trip home to visit his family. I gave him three or four weeks to get his stuff together and, if things were going well, I'd let him go home for a visit. My job was to stay in touch with him by phone. It was a long time before I finally got him on the phone, and then he says, "I got shot in the liver, you know the thing that makes you breathe."

"Oh, you mean the lung?"

He ended up putting someone in the trunk of a car. I think they were going to kill the guy, but the hostage was able to call out on a cell phone and the car got stopped while he was alive.

The Mexican kid got a long sentence for that. He was a young king in the gang, something that can come from being smart and being open to a high level of violence.

Another kid was part of a very powerful smart and violent Hmong gang. We joked that you could always tell if your home was broken into by a Hmong gang member because your kids' incomplete homework would be finished.

I was confirming this kid's home environment to see if he could return from Lincoln Hills School for Boys. I lined up a translator and went to the apartment, which was above a Hmong grocery store. As I was going up the stairs to the house, I read gang s**t all over the walls. There were 50-pound bags of rice at the top of the stairs.

His parents were older, traditional. They welcomed me. But I realized they did not know any English and probably did not know what the gang s**t meant other than to know it was not good. They did not take the signs down, maybe realizing the power the gang had. *Don't mess with them.* The translator was not there yet. So, the couple and I sat across the room from each other and smiled and laughed and giggled for an hour until the translator got there.

My father would say that the Hmong are beautiful, family-oriented people. After Vietnam, the U.S. made promises we did not keep. The CIA lied to the people. Have you seen the choppers on some of their fabric story arts? That is about the U.S. leaving them there after they had helped us. When we finally gave them acceptance to come to the U.S., the kids were made fun of in school. One of their ways to be cool was to form gangs for protection and assimilation. The Hmong people have a lot of pride. In many homes, you will see poster-size pictures of what the family did to help the Americans during the Vietnam war.

I wish the Hmong gang members could understand that assimilating into our culture is hurting them. We should all be emulating the kind and generous traditional Hmong culture.

THE DAY M WAS BORN

I'll never forget the day M was born.

Something told me to drive to Cedar Rapids to visit my cousin. First time ever. My cousin lived on the top floor of a big white house and as I climbed the stairs, I could hear her crying. I knocked on the door and she yelled, "Who is it?" You know, how they do in the hood.

"It's Joshua, your cousin," I yelled back. She is more like my sister than my cousin so when she saw me, she lit up. There was piles of dirty clothes and she quickly explained she didn't have any money for the Laundromat.

Her belly was huge with her pregnancy. She was having difficulty moving around and said she'd had a panic attack earlier. I could see both that she was depressed and that there were visual markings from a recent fight. When I asked, she said her boyfriend beat her up. She explained the fight like a battle-experienced vet, which she actually was. I had seen her knock out a man's tooth once and grab a woman by the hair, saying, "Bitch, I'll f**kin' kill you."

I was really pissed, though, that she was beat up. I wanted to get ahold of her boyfriend. To cool off, I suggested we get a bite to eat, and we went to the hole-in-the-wall restaurant where she had been waitressing.

The minute I took my first bite of food, I felt something hit my legs, like a whoosh. Her eyes went wide, and she got really pale. "Oh s**t, Joshua."

Chewing, I'm like, "What?"

She said, "My water just broke."

My cousin is a jokester, sick jokes. In my head I was saying, *You've got to be kidding. I'm not in this situation.*

"Your water broke? What the hell do you mean?" But I could tell she was in a real panic.

It was December. The roads were snowy. I told the people at the restaurant that I'd come back to pay my bill, but I had to get her out now, quick. As we drove, she put her legs on the dashboard. I was flying through the city but had no idea where anything was, so she was screaming out hospital directions. I ran into the hospital saying, "My cousin is giving birth."

We got her to a room, but she was alone. I had to stick around. I figured this had to be one of Grandmaw's jokes, from the other side. It was like her.

My cousin and I had been Grandmaw's favorites, I think, because we were both into a lot of s**t and she appreciated our wildness.

One time, my cousin was in Grandmaw's bathroom smoking a joint.

"Are you in there smoking?"

"No, Grandmaw, I'm not smoking."

"Well then, get the hell out because the house is on fire."

***

I hadn't even seen an animal birth before, but my cousin's contractions were getting closer together and I guess I was serving in the role of her man. Feeling like her big brother, I was telling her when another contraction was coming, and she was telling me, "F**k off."

It was a very, very emotional and exhausting experience. When M finally came out, it was obvious he was Black. The doctors and nurses were looking at me — I don't think they knew I was her cousin — waiting for an episode from the Jerry Springer show. Expecting pure drama.

Before he was born, she was calling the boyfriend. It was really irritating because he wanted him to be born that day, some sort of important family date. Instead of coming and helping the girl he had gotten pregnant, he was making phone calls. I finally grabbed my cousin's phone. "You need to get your ass up here."

When he got there, I said, "You made this f**kin' baby, you're going to watch this." But he only stayed a couple of minutes after M was born.

I promised myself that I was going to take responsibility for as much of M's life as I possibly could.

***

During one of those trips to see M, I saw that the guy who had been beating on her was gone and she was trying to make it on her own in a new apartment. No furniture. A few bags of fast food on the floor. I opened her cupboards. No food. None. But there was a bag of money in the freezer. She was holding it for somebody.

I said, "Let me do a few things; I've got to figure out how I'm going to take care of M."

She ended up saying, "Okay," and I took him with me. He couldn't walk yet and didn't have many words. On the drive, I was reciting stuff like, "The cat says..." "The cow says..." He would repeat some words, like cow and he would roar like a lion.

That night, I put him in bed with me because we didn't have a crib yet. I said my prayers and as I was looking at the ceiling, I kind of breathed out of my mouth, "Aw, f**k."

I thought he was sleep, but not. He clearly and quietly whispered, "It be okay."

A lot of stuff happened the year M and I lived in Rice Lake, Wisconsin, where my job had taken me. Not many Black or even mixed-race folks lived there, so when we went out, there were stares and stupid questions. I couldn't believe people had the audacity. One time, a Mennonite or Amish family stopped, then waited to ask me a question. "Is he your child?" It irritated me to the point where I asked them, "Does anyone ever ask why you wear those goofy-assed hats and bonnets?"

I felt bad after because I have respect for Amish beliefs and traditions. Now I realize they were just inquiring, and I've come to know there is no time for hate. Maybe I could have approached it differently and given them a learning moment.

There were a lot of firsts for me, acting as M's single parent. I potty-trained M. I taught him how to eat like a big boy. All of that. He even called me Dad.

My cousin, M's mom, had been a stripper at one point. It disgusted and saddened me that she felt she had to do such a thing. After I took M, I am almost 100% sure she got trafficked to Houston, Texas. When she got back, she got some type of burr in her ass and wanted her son back. The day I had to give him up, my dad said to me, "I know this is going to be hard; maybe one of the hardest things you have ever had to deal with, but you have to take him and return him to his mom. She is his biological mother."

I watched through my sliding glass window as my dad pulled away with M. I vomited.

I subsequently made many visits to Cedar Rapids, checking on them. My cousin was living with different people but never made the changes to her life to properly be a mother to M. From grade school through high school, M pretty much raised himself. As an adult, he was able to get a school janitorial job.

I don't believe any parent ever thinks, "I want the worst for my kid." I believe my cousin's intentions were great and that she really loved M. But she simply wasn't ready to raise a child. She hadn't worked on herself yet.

Today, she is addicted to drugs real bad and might be staying in a camper. Someone told me they seen her eating out of a garbage can. I promised my aunt I'd try to get her off the street. Prior to one visit, I could tell she was in a jam and hiding, running from someone. I actually wore a bulletproof vest.

Before I approach my cousin the next time, though, I'm studying the area online. I'll likely dress like a homeless dude and hang out just to get a feel for what's going on. She has been in trouble for quite some time.

I knew that getting into the corrections field was my purpose; that I would excel and be passionate about the work. As with my cousin, I understood, firsthand, what people could face with the pressures to act in damaging ways.

I also realize how the justice system puts many people under the same umbrella. Some have just made mistakes and should not be labeled as monsters. On the other hand, sadly, there are monsters out there who do need that disrepute.

ADULT GANG AND DRUG PAROLE OFFICER: WHAT WOULD YOU HAVE CHANGED OR DONE DIFFERENTLY?

I was desperate. I couldn't wait for my year to be up as a Serious Offender Juvenile Parole Officer in the Northwoods so that I could transfer to Madison to be closer to family and friends. I must admit that I was terrible with the organizing and paperwork. That was partly because of my ADHD, but mostly because of my need to help others in the trenches.

I have never looked at human beings as numbers and surely never want to sit at a desk typing and organizing files. I realize that is part of the job. However, if you are someone like me, you quickly see that if parole officer's paperwork functions were reduced and there was more time for mentoring, lives would be saved, and we would see a great reduction in recidivism numbers. This is one of the areas where we need criminal justice reform.

I transferred to the Department of Corrections Adult High-Risk Gang and Drug Unit in 2001 and was assigned a group of men convicted of gang and drug crimes. I remember when I first started and was being shown the ropes, I was so disappointed at all this paper pushing, knowing I'd be going absolutely nuts sitting and typing for hours. It would probably eventually lead me to being reprimanded.

However, the clients were exactly the people I wanted to serve, get to know, and assist in their life transformations. The position wasn't all bad. I loved doing home visits, discussions, and helping men during the worst times in their lives. I loved the contact, and I started to see my real purpose in life and within the Criminal Justice System.

One day, a coworker asked me to sit in on a meeting with a client who had violated his parole and was going to have to go into custody. We had to tell him about the custody and how law enforcement would come to pick him up.

He was a very large Black male. My partner and I were explaining his rule violation and consequences for his action. He got argumentative, which is normal, and we did a good job de-escalating him. He was cooling down when the two officers arrived with their chests puffed out and military-style direct strict demeanor. It set the client off again and he started to stand up. One of the officers pulled out his baton and banged the desk with it as if to say, "You are mine and you will obey me."

This took the client from about 20 to 100 real quick. The officers wrestled around with him and got him in custody, then took him off to jail.

A lot of things went through my head, later as I sat at my desk. The aggression had been unnecessary; we had the situation under control. If I were in that situation, parole officer or not, and an officer pulled out a baton on me when I am being somewhat peaceful, I might jump into fight mode as well.

Why not just use their trained verbal judo and treat him like an equal? The most powerful tool people have is their voice; their ability to communicate. This is something I was surely blessed with, maybe from being raised around all those adults. I say this because there are many former clients from the past 20 years who I consider friends and, believe me, those guys were roughnecks. I call them wild horses because many of them just needed the right guidance with a little love: true diamonds in the rough.

***

During this time, the Department of Corrections was renting a building near the Camp Randall Football Stadium on the University of Wisconsin–Madison campus where a lot of our clients were housed. I am guessing it had been student housing, but someone got the bright idea of stacking newly released individuals in efficiency apartments, with no supervision, except for surprise and scheduled home visits. Housing is a major issue when dealing with formerly incarcerated individuals, so on one hand a great idea, but next to a campus with nearly 44,000 students and no 24-hour monitoring, a train wreck.

A couple of my clients absconded from there and I can't blame them. It was like a low-rise housing project with men trying to work on themselves. I remember a child molester begging to be moved because he could hear children getting out of school and it was making him want to re-offend. Not good.

The campus building was filthy. It got so bad that one evening we met up with the Gang and Narcotics Task Force to do a sweep and check on clients. We all parked about a block away and discussed strategy. I agreed to walk up to the building with a plain-clothed officer to see if there were individuals hanging outside selling crack rock; there had been intel about that.

As the officer and I approached the building, someone whispered from the window, "Have you seen any police?" Guess whose room we hit first?

A lot of people do not realize the power the Department of Corrections has when it comes to clients. No warrants needed. We knocked and we could hear a lot of movement. This individual was a known sex offender. Once we got the door open, we quickly saw a young, under-age runaway girl sitting on the man's bed. This interaction had to have come from a higher power because the stage was set for a rape. He was taken into custody. That night we retrieved guns, stolen property, and drugs.

The building was a total set-up for failure, if you want my opinion. What do higher-ups think will happen when you put dozens of convicted felons together, in the heart of a city with no employment, very little mentoring, and a bag full of trauma? But make sure you get that paperwork done.

Makes me wanna holla.

***

At this time, I admitted to the Department that, like many of my clients, I had an ADHD diagnosis. I think they thought I was making up excuses about struggling with the paperwork. But it was real difficult.

I now realize that I could have done it but my position on seeing the need of helping these men in person was taking over in my mind. It was clear to me that the system was flawed or maybe, worse, it was set up this way to keep the criminal wheels in motion.

WHAT DOES IT MEAN TO BE HUMAN?

The parole officer paperwork continued to be overwhelming and was driving me nuts. The department's disability team began looking for positions that would fit me better. There were meetings with supervisors about my struggles; one supervisor took me to lunch telling me I was not cut out to be a parole officer. Even though I had a bachelor's degree, she said that my disability was getting in the way of the most important parts of the position. Her words cut deep and were discriminatory but stated so professionally that her meaning didn't dawn on me until I was alone. Wait, did I just get called dumb; professionally stupid? This was very embarrassing!

However, I don't think my struggles were only about me and my disability. I think some of it was about my beliefs and the great relationships I had with many of my clients.

I know that we all need someone to deal with us in a humane way. In my mind, parole officers should be cheerleaders and mentors. It is a teaching role; a way to uplift people rather than a babysitting role to maintain the status quo. Law enforcement has the privilege of being able to deal with people who are in terrifying and difficult situations. Done right, parole officers could be heroes for millions.

I know that most men and women who come out of prison don't want to go back, but their needs aren't always addressed or handled. Some are dropped off on a street corner with a box of their belongings, possibly wearing the wrong clothes for the season. They may have been locked up for decades and don't know how to use a cell phone or a computer or even read a bus schedule. They may have a check they cannot cash because they have no ID. They may need medications they cannot get. They are immediately told to go to Job Services (possibly across town) to look for work, take a UA (a urinalysis), meet curfew, and not hang out with known gang members or felons.

But suppose gang members are mislabeled. Suppose their family and friends have felonies but are also their connections and relationships—who they know from their past neighborhood. Formerly incarcerated people have a lot of pride. Trust is likely an issue. It is very hard to ask for help.

Being released is like stepping onto the surface of the moon. This is tough, but if they violate, they will get locked up again.

Maybe I am the only person in the world who feels this way but if you ask me, formerly incarcerated people are simply set up for failure. These guys can feel that the paperwork is more important than their lives; when you feel like you are just a number you can automatically go to feeling like giving up.

Yes, I do understand that officers play difficult roles that can leave them jaded with what they see and experience. But I was pulled more toward assisting these men with their needs than with worrying about locking them up for stupid-ass parole violations.

So, I enrolled in Correctional Officer Training School, which felt like it would be a better fit for me.

I entered training school as a sergeant and would be going to a minimum-security institution after graduation. I still had that zeal for helping others and couldn't wait to assist the men I would be working with. I wanted to think that everyone in the academy was there to make a difference in the lives of the men and women we would be looking after. I know I was excited because it was an opportunity to do what I like to do: meet people, get to know people, and assist them. I am my brother's keeper, no matter the circumstances. I always try to have this attitude.

My Correctional Officer Training School classmates were from all over Wisconsin. I instantly befriended a group of African Americans who would be working in the Milwaukee area. One of them was a preacher. I truly enjoyed him because I could tell he wanted to make a difference. He often led us in evening prayers.

Being sensitive to the topics of race from my upbringing and experiences at Loras College, I wondered how these future guards were going to do their jobs with very little knowledge of people who didn't look like them. It was clear that the Department of Corrections (DOC) had a hard time recruiting persons of color to work anywhere other than the Milwaukee, Kenosha, and Racine areas. If you were Black, would you want to work in basically White, small-town Waupun or Boscobel, Wisconsin? That would be a very tough decision for many families of color, if you ask me.

The other officers in training were mostly Whites from small towns. Much of their conversation was around state benefits, retirement, and overtime. Some seemed to be the type who had been bullied as kids. Now, with a badge and a radio, the bullied could become the bullies. Many were young with very little life experience; those who were older also came with a shared story. As farming and manufacturing decreased in Wisconsin, prisons became the new crop or production sites. You had White guys who had only looked at black and white cows their whole lives, taking the most stable job available to them in rural Wisconsin—prison guard.

I am not saying that the Whites were overtly racist, only that they were surely stepping into foreign lands. It worried me for several reasons. First was that their only history with other races likely came through television and negative biases. Second was that they were going to be working with hurt individuals enduring adverse circumstances, in very negative environments.

Our training was relatively generic around topics of race but was intense on defense tactics, shooting, verbal commands, and learning the inmates' con tactics used on staff. This was all good to know. However, we were being taught that inmates are all bad and that it's us against them. We learned to do cell shake-downs, human pat downs, and what to look for. We were sprayed with chemical agents and taught to shoot shotguns and rifles.

One of the most interesting days of instruction for me was when the Director of Training told his story of being held hostage during a prison riot, where individual officers were raped with shampoo bottles and inmates played a game with fire axes to see who could get the closest to an officer's bagged head. All bad, but the part of that training that stuck for me was the information that the DOC would not meet inmate demands for staff being held captive at any state institutions. That really made me think.

At least there was very little paperwork.

FROM PAROLE OFFICER TO PRISON GUARD

I didn't sleep much the night before my first evening on the job as a prison guard. I was assigned to a unit that had a bad reputation. Loud and wild. I ironed my uniform, shined my boots, and put on my cologne, which I had heard was a no-no, but I have been wearing cologne since preschool and I am not changing that. I am comfortable with myself as a man.

I was also excited because a captain who investigated Disruptive Groups (gangs) asked if I was interested in assisting with those duties in the institution. That was a "Yes." I have always had a passion for working with and understanding gangs. I understood a lot of the who, what, when, and why gangs are formed based on some of my upbringing and neighborhood relationships.

It turned out that my childhood babysitter's big brother was currently doing life behind bars for his role in nationwide gangland murders. He was charged under the RICO law (Racketeer Influenced and Corrupt Organizations Act). If you are a gang member and reading this, you'd better learn what RICO is real quick. Also, familiarize yourself with what a correctional system "G Card" is; it might make you think twice about your next tattoo.

So, there I was, in the parking lot, getting ready to walk into the prison my first night on the job. The officers gathered near the control center for roll call and a briefing on institutional happenings within the last 24 hours. One thing I already knew I didn't like was the sound of the heavy, steel entrance door closing. The sound was that of permanency, even for someone who gets to go home.

Everyone was scrambling to get on the overtime sheet. I had heard a rumor that there were guards making over $100,000 a year by utilizing the overtime. It was based on seniority. I think you could tell which people did all that overtime because they looked messy, disheveled, and tired. Some of these guys are good people—family men and so forth—but if they are tired, getting angry and frustrated, with bad eating habits, that kind of exhaustion isn't fair to the inmates who are vulnerable human beings.

For rookies like me, getting jammed didn't come with additional pay. "Getting jammed" is being ordered to stay for another eight hours because the next shift called in sick. One of the worst feelings is hearing the phone ring when its five minutes to quitting and the captain says, "You must stay!" Not a morale booster at all.

"You mean to tell me that I been in this hot box, smelling this s**t, listening to this all evening, and now I have to spend the night here?" Gets old quick. But those night shifts were times I learned the most from the men, even with their character flaws. They are true teachers, educators on life. It only requires the time to listen.

Compare these structures—overtime and getting jammed—to how firefighters work. They stay at the fire station for the days they are working. They get the rest they need. They are properly hydrated and eating well. They are ready for emergency situations.

Prison guards are not bad people, but they have put themselves in a bad place. The levels of suicide, PTSD, alcoholism, drug misuse, heart attacks, and strokes—all exacerbated by an endemic culture of machismo—are extremely high. Officers either let their work break their hearts open or let those hearts harden. I know some officers who have quit because they feared the latter.

An inmate driver picked us up in a golf cart after roll call. Some of the units were a distance away, behind the fences. The driver instantly said, "You're new" and "Good luck" with a little chuckle. I thanked him for the ride and entered my unit. An old, squeaky, screen door slammed behind me, letting everyone know I was there for shift change. A big barn fan blew air down the hall. It was sticky, hot, and the floors were sweaty. Everyone was locked down for the shift change.

The first person I saw was a short, muscular White man with his head shaved bald. He was looking through his window, studying me. Everyone was sizing me up as a man.

The unit was two stories high with an office on the ground floor for the sergeant, who didn't say much as we traded places. He handed me a list of the inmates' names and told me who was out working their job.

COUNT TIME!!!

Counting inmates is one of the most important concentrations within an institution for obvious reasons. I grabbed my name list and began my first walk, peeking into each window to count the men.

I was nervous on that first walk and thinking how lucky I was to not be in one of them rooms. In the cells, men were sleeping, listening to music, watching TV, working out, painting, staring into space, or joking around with their cellmates. This walk was a slow stroll because I was introducing myself to those who wanted an introduction. I was being mindful of my posture, how I spoke, and surely my eye contact. I was studying their stature, strength, intelligence, age, and vulnerability levels. There were African Americans, Native Americans, Puerto Ricans, Mexicans, Italians, and one Russian.

A very large Native American man told me that later that night he needed to sit in the cafeteria and record a book on tape for Madison College students with disabilities. He shared a room with another Native American who was drawing tattoo art. They were two very talented and intelligent men.

My next stop was at a Black Muslim's room where he was just finishing up prayer. I noticed his Qur'an was placed on some form of stand, which I found to be interesting. This individual had art all around his cell and when I tell you it was good, I mean it was extraordinary. His talent was portraits, and you could not tell if they were drawings or photos.

After that first walk, I called my count into the communication center. All inmates must be accounted for. After the numbers come in, the control center announces over the radio/walkie talkie that the count is clear. It is then the sergeant's job to let the inmates know. I found out quickly that it is very important that when you let the men know, you must do so in a manner that is loud so everyone can hear. It is done with a loud, "Couuuuuuunt is cleeeeeeear."

A Black man with very deep voice told me that I had to get louder. I explained that my voice was not loud; it doesn't carry. I told him, "Whenever I am on duty, you can be my spokesperson." He asked if he could yell "Count clear" right now and I said, "Go ahead." He yelled it out. In an instant, I could tell that hadn't been done before. The inmates were waiting to hear my voice rather than one of their own. I don't think they could believe that I allowed it to happen. Pretty certain I broke a rule on my first day, but it surely was an icebreaker!

During count time, my two kitchen workers—an old White man and a young Black man—were in the kitchen preparing the unit dinner, which came on a delivery truck. They had been locked in the kitchen during count. Our first meal together was baked chicken, salad, and one slice of cake. I set up my desk towards the back of the room so the kitchen workers could check in with me after the inmates received their trays. Here they came, loud and messing with each other about the latest handball game, domino match, basketball, and horseshoes. Buddies.

As they took their seats, which were not assigned, they separated. Blacks over here, Natives over there, Latinos in their own spot, and Whites had their grouping. Race played a role in where they sat. I quickly realized the same was true on the rec yard, the track, and in picking teams for basketball. It was my first visual of prison politics.

I was interested in this dynamic and I later asked a few individuals of different races what would happen if I assigned seating with every other seat a different color or race. I received multiple answers like, "Good luck with that," "No f**king way," "That won't happen," "F**k that."

I hadn't said I was going to do that, but I did use it as leverage, letting them know that I wanted a smooth-running unit where everyone was included and that if I felt we were not getting along I might follow through and seat them by color. I was letting them know that I didn't play racism from any angle.

That first meal was a little overwhelming for me, but I learned who I had to keep an eye on: who was mature, who was immature, who was vulnerable from mental illness, who was weak, and who had the power and control. It was clear that the long timers—the men who had been locked up for long periods of time—were the men I was going to be learning from because they carried themselves in a considerate manner and were respected by others. That institution was their home. I was just a visitor.

I never took this prison guard job with the intention of making other people's lives harder. I wanted to learn from them and have them learn from me, as men. I wanted them to remember me as a man they could trust and who carried himself as a brother.

I am not your enemy, not your counter, not your watchdog.

If you work in an institutional setting, you may hear the term "inmate lover" thrown around a lot. It's usually directed, by employees, at those who care for the population and want the best for them, understanding that they are human. I probably got labeled as an "inmate lover" that first evening for even being interested in the lives of the men I was supervising.

I am not perfect and there were inmates who got on my nerves. Some things started to bother me that I wouldn't have expected. I got sick of hearing them bones (dominos) cracking on the table across from my office (they need to make nerf dominos for prisons). I got sick of hearing all the bulls**t talk and glorification of criminal behavior. I got sick of smelling dirty asses. Have you ever smelled a fiery fart in an environment that is sticky and hot, knowing that every man just ate the same thing? Marinate on that for a minute.

Yes, I broke up fights, sent men to the hole, and got played. I do believe in punishment when necessary. But what is beautiful is that I took a bad situation and learned about some remarkable people who were incarcerated. Not much separated me from them and it was so clear from hearing some of their stories that I could have easily been their roommate at times of my life. The only difference was that they got caught.

I met short-timers and lifers. Killers and robbers. I met teddy bears and monsters. I met very smart men and men who were victims of failed educational systems. I met men I could see myself hanging out with on the outside and men I hoped never crossed my path again. I learned we are all men and that our walks differ based on circumstances.

I understood that officers play difficult roles that can leave them jaded with what they see and experience. There are good officers and bad officers, some who need to be there and others who shouldn't. Like anywhere else, there are some people who walk among us like cancer cells. I knew instantly that those who used the "inmate lover" lingo were individuals I needed to stay away from.

My first month at the institution, I heard an officer mumble, "Let that motherf**ker die, one less for us to count," as others were trying to cut away a bed sheet from around an inmate's neck and resuscitate him.

There had been a disturbance on another unit. I heard it over the radio, but word travels quicker than a radio in a prison. The man was hauled off to the hole. One would like to think he was being punished for stabbing someone, fighting, or breaking s**t. But that wasn't it. He got taken to segregation because he was on the phone when he wasn't supposed to be. He was wishing his five-year-old son a happy birthday. The officer who sent him to the hole was the first person I heard calling another officer "inmate lover."

As I was leaving to go home that night, the emergency alarms sounded on our radios. They needed a response to segregation. A man hanging!

"Segregation" is a place where you can feel, smell, and taste the darkest side of life and when something like this happens, that air fills with a thick aroma. What is that? What do you call it? Is it the smell of fear? The smell of death? Or is it just the smell of the end of the struggle? I don't know, but it's there.

As we all entered the seg tomb, the female officer-in-the-bubble (a safety pod for officers) was standing at the window yelling which way to run. I learned something in about two seconds that I don't remember being taught in the academy. The sergeant-in-the-bubble can only open a cell on the order from a white shirt (captain or lieutenant). There wasn't one there yet. Officers were screaming, "Pop it," but she couldn't. She was following orders. Alarms were sounding, radios chattering, men in other cells screaming, and pounding on their doors. Adrenaline blows out the top of your head.

And, ironically, everything slows down at the same time. You remember it all, in detail, as if your mind were a recording device that you didn't know you had.

Was everyone experiencing this detail? Everything amplified? Were the inmates experiencing this with us? And, more importantly, was the man in distress experiencing this? Because if he was, the last words he heard besides, "Come on, wake up." was "Let that motherf**ker die, one less to count."

That is wrong!

FOOTBALL—NFL TRYOUTS:
NO WOULDA, COULDA, SHOULDA FOR ME

There I was. Twenty-nine years old. I was working in a prison thinking, "This isn't what I want to be doing with my life." The mature prisoner I'm working with—human to human—says, "You don't belong here. How old are you? What was your ultimate goal?"

"I wanted to become a punter."

"Well, go get it."

So I quit my job as a prison guard and pursued being an NFL punter.

I began researching what I would have to do to reach that point. Who were the best coaches and evaluators?

I met a world-renowned guru, kicking coach, and author/inventor. I met him in Minnesota where we punted under a sports dome. He had scientifically figured out how to punt and kick, like a mad scientist.

Then there was an evaluation camp at Purdue. If they thought you had what was needed there, you could start training at the University of Nevada–Reno. I was fine-tuning, learning the techniques, and answering questions I had when I talked with my football as a teen.

At training in Reno, there were young kickers from the University of Alabama, LSU, Penn State, and more. I was a grandpaw compared to them. They called me "Old School." The first time I was out there, I was not prepared and was still getting my steps down. I took home what I learned but did not make the cut.

Just being around these like-minded individuals was total heaven for me. One time, I went to take a piss and realized the guy to my right was a well-known NFL special team coach and to my left was a guy who had played in a Super Bowl. I told myself, I am among them right now! We all gotta do the same thing. They don't know what I'm feeling —pissing between two greats.

The sport's agent for Jim Leonhard (Jimmy Leon-Hard, the nickname given to him by his players) told me he was going to let me have some fun kicking at Camp Randall Stadium when the Ravens special teams coach and recruiter were there. We had perfect weather and I was killing the ball. I had been training with an NFL ball. Jim brought out smaller college balls to practice. I was kicking the s**t out of them. Day of the trial, there was wind in Camp Randall and my punts weren't the greatest, but alright.

The college coach asked if I had any eligibility left. But my dumb ass had previously signed a pro contract, so I could not play college ball. I would have had four years of eligibility. They did let me come to practices and evaluate punters, at a distance.

I began to realize I wasn't going to make it at the professional level. I was feeling bad, and yet remained encouraged. I realized it was really important to have an A-to-Z plan for life. I was seeing the greatness around me. At one time, I might have made it. But I am content now knowing that I am not a member of the *woulda, coulda, shoulda* club. I answered that question for myself. I tried.

If you are a young man and you gave up, that living-in-the-past-s**t is for the birds. You *coulda*. You didn't. You *shoulda*. You didn't. Nobody wants to hear about you *woulda*.

PRISONER RE-ENTRY AND THE MADISON-AREA URBAN MINISTRY (MUM), DBA JUST DANE

Being a prison guard had been my third job within the Department of Corrections, and again, I knew, I didn't belong. Still not right.

I understand security. I understand law and I surely know prisons are not filled with choir boys, but I also know that the mission should always be public protection and rehabilitation.

In front of my mother, I took an oath with pride that I would serve and protect our community from individuals who have harmed society. But if rehabilitation is not in the cards, then what the f**k are we doing?

I had tried out for professional football and that door had closed.

So, I took a job as head of security for a major data center that was filled with computers and could withstand a level-five tornado strike. Clients showed up in million-dollar cars; one guy had a microchip embedded in his arm that held all his financial data and additionally started his car!

My job there? Keep my mouth shut and walk the complex every hour. The job was important and very slow moving. My supervisor agreed that I could study for (and complete) my master's degree in criminal justice while on the job. I did and graduated from the University of Phoenix online.

At the same time, a friend told me about Madison Area Urban Ministry (MUM), so I volunteered with their prisoner reentry circles. I enjoyed working with the returning prisoners—people returning to the community from prisons or jails -- helping them create a new life on the outside.

Then a TIA stroke changed my path. I realized I had to have another open-heart surgery. I feared dying. At the same time, my daughter's mom was pregnant. I became a father and a few months after her birth, I had the surgery. I wanted to live for our daughter; to be her dad.

(Shortly, I'll introduce you to my daughter, Joshlynn. You'll love her!!)

I quit the security position and took a full-time job with MUM. One thing is certain. MUM shaped me into the man I am today. The experiences with that organization taught me to understand human need.

Much like my father's encounters at the NSA Da Nang hospital during Vietnam, I was now receiving casualties in a hot zone. I know many might not like that comparison because we are not in an official war on our homeland streets and in our prisons, but the damage done to peoples' minds is surely comparable.

When I was younger, I admit I held the same view many people do: *Lock them up and throw away the key.* But MUM taught me that today's former inmates are tomorrow's neighbors. No one is only the worst thing he or she has ever done.

MUM also taught me about my White privilege. It educated me on the vicarious trauma that counselors and mentors can experience. I believe all new criminal justice hires should do internships at a place like MUM so they can put faces on and see the humanity of the people they are arresting, guarding, and supervising.

Relationships started quickly at MUM. Mostly out of desperation. Don't ever let someone tell you they have seen or heard it all because they haven't. Triage helping centers like MUM will show you that in a heartbeat! Smiles, hugs, and encouragement are real, but MUM is also a place where the gorilla of life dumps off its victims and many tears are shared. Everyone who comes through the MUM door has a story and at the end of the day, you are left thinking to yourself, *You can't make this s**t up. It is live, uncut, unedited. The pulse of the streets is in your face.*

No one is better than anyone else. Everyone is accepted, loved, and treated as brother and sister, regardless of their life circumstances. Relationships are developed, trust is earned, and love is produced. People helping people.

FOOTBALL—COLIN KAEPERNICK

Brothers and Sisters, I am not saying I have the answers to anything our world throws at us, but I am taking a knee because I want to dialogue peacefully.

This White boy knows why #7, perhaps one of the greatest quarterbacks of all time, respectfully took that knee on the football field, during the national anthem, before all of us.

For our professional athletes to turn their backs on one of the best quarterbacks you could ask for and not hire Kaepernick shows me that sports are not always a place where racism doesn't exist. It appears it does exist and even at a high level. What about brotherhood?

I was disappointed in some who turned their heads on Kaepernick when he took that knee.

I don't understand what was wrong with him taking a knee. I have knelt to football and baseball coaches, to children, to church leaders, and before God. It is the humblest form of non-speech etiquette you could possibly give our world.

You know why?

RESPECT. Respect for all humans.

Kaepernick's silent protest was nothing more than a plea. He was simply seeking the wellbeing of all humans. He was trying to wake us the f**k up! It was one of the most patriotic gestures I have ever witnessed.

I realize that, by putting this in my book, I am going to catch a lot of s**t. So be it.

NONSTOP PEOPLE AT MUM'S DOOR

When I say respect for all humans, I mean every human being on the planet, like the nonstop people who come through MUM's doors. People from all walks of life, showing their many beautiful hues. In the trenches, the last thing on a person's mind is color. In the trenches, people are literally trying to survive. Some are fighting inexplicable, but real, battles.

These people, these casualties, are mostly wounded men and women coming out of our criminal justice institutions. Some mental wounds are minor so a little pressure on the wound is what is needed. But the vast majority are critical and bleeding profusely.

What war did they come from? What started their struggles?

Pause and consider these stories of a few of my brothers and sisters, the nonstop people who came through MUM's swinging door.

Depending on how you were raised and your life experiences, you may not even realize these are American stories. But they are. You are in America, my friend. The other one! An America that needs to look in the glass and tell us all if she likes what she sees staring back.

Dear A:

The people from your student loan finally quit blowing up my phone! Apparently, they didn't realize that you died. I had no idea that you used me as a reference. Lol! You had to be one of the funniest, skinniest women I ever met in my entire life. I remember the day you had me laughing so f**king hard and as I was laughing you said under your breath, "Bernie Mac ain't got no s**t on me." Funny! You know what? No offense to Bernie Mac but I think she was on to something.

A, why do so many people from Chicago use phrases like Boowopda Bam and Joe Sausage Head?

"I don't know no BooWopda Bam or no motherf**kin' Joe
Sausage Head but I do know Hootie Who and Run Dumb
Dumb!
 You was funny! I am so sorry that I wasn't there with you on
the day that you died. I wish you would have just called. You
had my office and cell number. We just discussed their
persistence. We discussed greed and money. We even
discussed genocide!

You looked pretty at your funeral. I kissed your forehead and
held your hand while you and I prayed. I always loved your
hugs, sis. Believe it or not they made me feel good too. There
were a lot of new faces at your funeral, people I didn't know.
Not to sound funny or be disrespectful but I have to tell you
something and keep it real just as you do with me.

After I gave you my final kiss and was walking out of the
sanctuary full of people the back of my hair stood up. My
streetar, my fight or flight, turned on. What were you telling
me? Were you telling me that the person or persons that sold
you your last dose were in that room? Were you telling me to
be careful in the jungle? What was it?

I had to readjust my train of thinking and just pull away
knowing that I lost a friend today and that she is in a better
place. Honestly, mind went south, and I wanted to find out
which motherf**king dope dealer was standing in line to look
at your body! That's that f**king fake love we was talking
about, I know the pussy was in there! And that is why I am
writing this book so that your voice is heard!

But as you said to me one day, "It's all in the game."

When will people learn that this is not a f**king game, A? It's about peace, love, and happiness. It's about loving someone deeper and being my brother's keeper!

Love you!!!
Your Brother

***

I was at a gas station and some guys pulled up and were talking s**t to this girl I liked a lot. They had a gun in the car, and I told them that if they hadn't had that I would have whipped them right then for talking like that. Back and forth.

A couple of days later, this girl came to my office. She had been trying to do better for herself. But now her eyes were swelled shut, her lip was split, and she was almost crippled. She was asking for help. I'm like, "What happened?" She told me the guy's name who hurt her and, when I looked him up, it was the same guy I got into it with at the gas station. Several guys had held her hostage and raped her for days until her disability check came in. Then they made her withdraw the money. It makes you really upset.

***

D, this next part of the book is for you, my brother. I know big things were coming your way. You were determined to have change in your life. I appreciated your comment, "You are the coldest White boy on the planet!" I appreciated all our conversations, stories, and even heartfelt interventions. You taught me a lot about the streets and life, big bro.
The stuff you taught me was critical to saving my own life and you were right in saying, "These streets are a motherf**king jungle that doesn't do s**t but cause pain." They say the game don't change, only the players. That's a bunch of bulls**t!!! This motherf**ker a cold world, your death showed me that.

I'm still looking out for your sister. We all are. I made her crack up laughing at an event in Penn Park. She using a walker now and a wheelchair. She got the benefits she deserved and has a roof over her head, sober and a joy to be around. Whenever I see her, we hug and then start talking about you.

A few days after you died, she told me that you said she could trust me. Did you know this was coming? You even told her not to be around and ironically, she told Yaqub and me to keep it quiet on how it all played out. She said if your brothers found out they would kill everyone involved. You didn't want that to happen.

Everything good. All is well with my family! This for you bro......Love you

***

It was around Christmas when I first met D. I remember because he brought some very expensive candies and gave them to my female co-workers to wish them Merry Christmas. You could tell he was the guy everyone loved.

When we got back to work after Christmas break, he was the first guy through the door. D was such a survivor. He knew how to get his needs met and there were days he met with everyone at MUM, in our separate offices, each person doing something for him. A cold hustler!

After a year of working with him, right around that next Christmas, he came stumbling into MUM during a snowstorm. He was carrying a nice peacoat and a bag with some home-cooked food he had made somewhere.

He was so excited to tell me that the coat was for me, to give me a business look, he said. I thanked him. He had also cooked me a nice steak and some potatoes at someone's apartment. It was delicious.

I asked him where he had gotten my gifts and was told he saw the coat on the bus and figured it was about my size. And the steak? Well, he once found a butcher's apron at the Dig and Save Store. He wore that when he would go into grocery stores and stand near the meat counter. At the right moment, he would take meat and put it in his pants, to the side. "It would stick to my legs," he said. And then he would walk out of the store. I had to laugh. (Later he took a steak to one of my co-workers and I simply could not tell her the rest of the story.)

D was in such a good mood and smiling so hard. He sat next to me as I ate my food. We listened to some music. He knew I was thankful for the gifts.

Out of the blue, he asked, "Why do you want to be on the south side of Madison, helping a bunch of Black convicts?"

Not all our clients were Black, but they did make up a large percentage. My answer was pretty clear to him about why I work on the south side and it was at this point we were no longer professional and client, but brothers.

Over time, he told me his deepest darkest secrets, none of which I will discuss.

He told me about his dreams, what made him tick, and where he got the scars he was wearing. He battled addiction, homelessness, literacy, institutionalization, and love. He did not know what to do with love or affection because he feared believing they was true. That it was real.

He was from a big family who had migrated from Atlanta to Chicago, and then to Wisconsin. He wore distinct markings and scaring on parts of his body and face that were from a life of trauma. One tragic burn scar was from a moonshine-still fire. His father had him and a few of his many siblings at the still one day and someone tipped something over. The fire traveled quickly. One of his siblings died in that fire.

The family migrated to Chicago and lived in very poor conditions. D hit the streets young and joined a gang for protection, community, and money. Raw survival made it almost impossible for any formal schooling other than street education.

One day, he and I were walking to the courthouse for his hearing. A blind man got off the bus and D said hello to him. The blind man didn't laugh as he said, "D, you stay out of my pockets." D did laugh.

It was at the hearing that I realized D couldn't read. As we waited for his turn in the courtroom, he asked me, "Do you want a doughnut?" When he got back, he smiled, saying, "I got you a Danish, brother," and when I asked where he got it, he cracked up laughing. "I used to work here. I know this place like the back of my hand."

"Well, where did you get it?"

Another laugh, "The judge's area."

So, yes, I took part in a theft with him because we sure did eat the judge's doughnuts.

D had served time in Illinois Stateville Correctional Center. His cellmate was one of Chicago's biggest gang leaders and D was the guy's head of security.

D and I were working on everything to revamp his life. His sister had moved up from Atlanta to be with him and he encouraged her to seek help through MUM. She had cut a man's penis. In her orientation, I watched her tell the story to a co-worker and when she said she cut it at the root, my co-worker slowly, subconsciously, closed his legs. I had to laugh at him. She said, "The motherf**ker thought I was playing, and he said, 'Bitch, I know karate.'"

Her verbal response when he woke up fast?

"N****, I know crazy.'"

We were working on getting D into rehab. I didn't think he was using but one day he still had some white stuff in his nose. It stood out because his skin was so dark. When I asked if he had been using, he denied it. But when I handed him a mirror, he apologized, and we began the process of finding rehab for him.

Several days later, our CEO brought the staff together and with a heavy voice and heart told us D had been found dead in a church closet. "Drug overdose" was what they said.

I lost a brother that day, our entire office did. A brother. I miss him! We miss him!

These are some of the beautiful people, formerly incarcerated, I met while working at MUM:

- A teacher who suffered from childhood trauma and had problems with alcohol and driving while drinking.

- A prison psychologist whose vicarious trauma was amplified by listening to yall's lives and crimes.

- A retired professional boxer who lost track of himself when his cherished father passed.

- Two men who were locked up from age 12 and released in their 30s.

- A White dude who was moving kilos.

- A homeless former welder with a rotten heel ulcer that smelled like roadkill.

- A greedy HVAC technician who thought he was saving money by selling cocaine.

- A pimp who cared about his prostitutes' teeth.

- A prostitute with a real cool (real) name who looked like a movie star. She was young, fresh, and first time in someone's stable. She wanted to be a teacher but couldn't afford school.

- A former gang leader, my father's age, who cried when talking about today's kids and gangs. When asked why he was crying, he'd say, "It wasn't supposed to be like this. I took part in creating it, but we created monsters. They lied. Even if a dad is living a street life—feeling s**tty about himself and doing bad things—he still need to be around his kid. That kid don't look at his dad like he is a villain; he or she is looking up to the father. He can still be a bad dude and be a good dad who keep the gang stuff away from family."

- A kid who called his mother a "cum dumpster." Later, he sent me an email saying he had spit another man's sperm into my coffee. His mom was a prostitute who had turned tricks in front of him when he was a baby.

- A 19-year-old drug dealer who said that rapper Lil Wayne didn't have s**t on him when it came to money. He wasn't lying.

- A radio DJ.

- Two clients on the same day; one of them had killed the other's daddy. Oops on my end!

- A former pimp who did over 20 years in prison. He was raised by a pimp. Today he is out trying to help his people and asking for forgiveness.

- A carpenter who suffered head injuries from football and couldn't stay away from crack rocks and scams. He is a great fisherman, doing well, married, raising children, and still fishing.

- Many barbers who learned the trade while incarcerated.

- Chefs who used to like to cook cocaine.

- A former football great who hung out with big-name rappers when cocaine was big in Miami.

- An aging Black man who wanted me to speak with his wife and family about the voices he heard. He feared they would not like him and call him crazy. I saw him a few weeks ago: homeless and talking to himself.

- An abused woman who still sucked her thumb.

- A lot of snitches. I personally couldn't believe it, but there are a lot and all with the same story, "I got to be here for my family."

- A cool dude who restored cars for celebrities but got caught up in the cocaine trade. One day, he didn't look well, and I recognized the look. He had to have open-heart surgery.

- A dude who walked away from the hospital after getting into it with the police. They found him a few days later, fetal position in the home he grew up in. Dead.

- A very smart young lady struggling to find meaningful employment. Never been in trouble. Eyes full of tears, she asked for money for a flight down south, or a bus ticket. "What's wrong?" "My twin brother was killed at a gas station. He just got a teaching job. Killed over a f**kin car. Mannnnnn."

- A biker who couldn't quit driving his bike while drunk, for nobody! He started drinking heavily when his girlfriend died of cancer. I convinced him to let me give him a haircut and beard trim to get him in the door at a job. He had motorcycle parts in his living room. After the haircut he said, "Awwww, f**k, I look like a banker." He got the job.

- A man they called Haaaalaaaaayluia because he gave his life to God. Many agreed he was one of the worst inmates our system has seen; it would take an entire squad to get him down. He spent years in the hole, naked and cold. After my heart surgery, this man was there, praying over me in the hospital.

***

Gibson blew into the MUM office one day, talking constantly, all hyper and energetic. Ever since I'd known him, he was homeless, but interestingly, he always wore his Golden Gloves prize-fighting medallion. He would regularly get revoked while on parole and would leave that medallion with me for safe keeping.

There is an Iowa elementary school named after his grandmother for her efforts to introduce Black history in Cedar Rapids schools. The state NAACP gives an annual "Yes, I Can" award in her honor.

Gibson's father was his boxing coach. Here was a boy with this dream but when his father died, Gibson spiraled out of control and got into the streets. I fear there are too many kids like this out there.

Working with Gibson through MUM, I worried about him living in the streets—once with an older woman, a dog, and a cat—all in one vehicle. Gibson was not allowed to do anything with his hands, which were both lethal and connected with his crime. But boxing was what he wanted to do; teaching kids to box their way out of whatever they were in.

Gibson is a good guy and I considered asking him to move in with me at one point, but the collision of our two ADHDs wouldn't have been positive. Maybe now he is beginning to see what a beautiful human being he is since being off parole and trying new things like fishing for catfish.

***

I met so many people at MUM that it doesn't even make sense! It's crazy that as I chose to write this today as the news flashed that DMX had died. I was listening to DMX's track "Slipping." It helped me through this portion.

I loved each of these individuals who all belonged to one race—the human race. Their skin tones were all beautiful and unique. In this life and hopefully into the next, they are all considered family. This is what Brothers look like!!!!!

***

About six months before I left MUM for what I am doing now—gang intervention work—I was leading a boy's group with John and Yaqub. We were working with a gang group, something we knew well. After working with adults, we got this, right? No problem. The game don't change, only the players, remember?

Shiiiiiiit, an entirely different world and not at all what I expected! Clique names were crazy, they had numbers in members and were completely involved in all kinds of gang crimes. I realized quickly, from my educational standpoint, that I was witnessing the beginning stages of a gang. The incubation process was almost over. Soon they would show me why that old gang head (my MUM client) shed those tears for assisting in gang creation.

What goes on in group stays in group. That was our main rule, and I am going to keep it at that.

But a few things I will tell you about the group members is that they were all little boys, all beautiful human beings who suffered from trauma and other things like ADHD and separation disorder. Each of them had a unique story to tell and each of them was eager to find a way to express himself.

- "Drill Music?"
- "My little brother and I got twin Glocks?"
- "When I do my first bit, I am ......?"
- "Im fin Ball in Paradise?"
- "I will take care of my momma when I play in the NFL or NBA."
- "I got bars, man. I am going to be a rap artist."

Sadly, today, some of them are in prison, some are homeless, one is a pimp, some are dead. Each of them will always be known as a gang member.

And each of them will always be loved by me.

Did you just read what I wrote about boys expressing themselves? It amazed me. I spent all those years working with adults and now everything that I thought was going on, wasn't. I knew that if I was going to make any impact in this life, I needed to get to these kids. Who the f**k is teaching them this s**t? These are little boys and should be talking about girls, homework, sports, music anything but drugs, f**king, money, and gang violence.

* * *

I remember at our first meeting, Yaqub and I were more perplexed than surprised by what we were hearing. I am not sure if he said this in front of the boys or just to me so they couldn't hear but I remember him saying something that will stick with me for the rest of my life, and I hope this is his quote because someone deserves credit for it.

"This is f**ked up, my brother, but hear me out. Imagine you and I are standing by a fast-moving stream, camping, okay?, when one of us notices a bunch of kids caught in the current and they are speeding past us and screaming for help—or floating by dead! What are we going to do?"

Me: "Get a rope, jump in, and find a way to save them."

Yaqub: "Exactly. We will die! Why don't we walk upstream and see who the monster is that's throwing them in the water and take care of him?"

Many adults I met at MUM had lives that were so jacked up. I wanted to get to the preventive side; to work more with kids. I was helping people at MUM but felt I had to do more to stop this earlier. If we all tried to jump in that water, change wouldn't happen. We all need to get ahead of the now, now, now. Somebody needs to be working on the back game of what causes poverty, negative race relations, all of it.

But then life intervened in both beautiful and traumatic ways.

JOSHLYNN'S BIRTH: NOVEMBER 3, 2009

I will never forget the day that Joshlynn's mom asked me to meet her at a family restaurant in DeForest, near Madison. "We have to talk," she said. I was a little nervous about the conversation because I could hear a tremble of desperation in her voice. To be very honest, we really didn't know each other that well.

We met like two teenagers at a dance, but it wasn't a dance. It was at the stoplight, right next to Camp Randall Stadium. I drove past the stadium every day on my way to work. I still had enough love for the game of football in me that seeing that field gave me a feeling of encouragement in life.

She was just getting off from UW Hospital and Clinics where she worked as a registered nurse.

At the time, I was living with a beautiful, strong woman from the islands of Trinidad and Tobago. Her father was a captain on a boat that took workers out to sea each day to work the oil fields. She and I were the closest of friends. She was very mature for her age and intrigued by the sciences. She graduated from Edgewood College and was doing research on the human papilloma virus (HPV). Daily, we had intellectual conversations, took long walks, cooked together, and, man, did we laugh a lot. Her accent cracked me up, especially when she got upset. We loved each other and needed each other for support.

At one point, we were literally living in a closet and sharing a bathroom with many other men and women. It was a dirty, nasty, cockroach-infested environment that even warranted the weekend presence of the Guardian Angels, who had branched out from protecting the New York City subway system to any communities with challenges, like Madison at that time.

We lived next to a tiny Mexican dude who didn't know much English. He worked full-time at a State Street restaurant. At night, you could hear him making noise in his closet space. He was building toys for store displays: a second job. His family lived in terrible, deadly poverty in Mexico and he was sending money back.

One day, he knocked at the door. His only words were: smells, infection, and come. I thought he was going to tell me that he had an infection that smelled but he pointed to another neighbor's apartment space. As I walked to the door, I instantly understood why he said smells, but it was not an infection. It was a smell I knew. I told him it was a dead body stinking up our hallway. The police came and then the coroner. The guy left zipped up in a body bag. He had taken a fatal dose of heroin.

My strong woman and I were there for each other. I remember one time she called me when she was walking home from work. A White man was following her and then, somehow, he found a way to get ahead of her. She thought he was gone but when she approached an open garage door, he was standing there, pants around his ankles, masturbating while looking at her.

Calling the police was not her first response; she called me. I told her to hang up and call 911. The police arrived and arrested him.

A few months later, we attended his court hearing and I sat in the courtroom to support her. The court made her describe the events and discuss body parts, a very humiliating procedure. I could tell he was some rich White boy who could do no wrong. His mother lied for him saying he couldn't have done it because he was at her house during that time, eating his favorite dish—spaghetti.

Months before, two other female students had filed a complaint on him saying he masturbated in front of the car they were sitting in.

As court went on, my girlfriend was strong, but also scared. When his family and attorney started lying on his behalf, I called the man a f**king bitch. I did not think the judge could hear, but I was told to shut my mouth, or I would have to leave the court. I sat quiet the rest of the hearing. The man's punishment was to stay off campus and no longer attend the college.

A few months later, she and I were out for a walk and as we turned down an alley, she froze. Three men were walking toward us, and she leaned in and said, "The one in the middle is the man who did that."

I could sense her victimization and trauma. "Do you want to say something to him? It is okay, you are with me." I hate seeing people hurt and when I feel trapped, cornered, insulted, or I see someone hurting or being bullied, I can go from 0 to 100 real quick.

The privileged pervert said something to his buddies, and they laughed. I yelled, "Hey, bitch, do you remember me? Yah, YOU bitch. Do the three of you want a piece of me?"

On the streets, you become an expert in reading body language. I knew, at this point, I had the upper hand. They were in a situation their privilege couldn't get them out of. They already knew I'd whoop the dog s**t out of all three of them and wasn't afraid to go to jail for this one. I was disgusted by the whole process. I had gone to 100!

I could see my girl's confidence and power as a woman mount up and told her it was okay to let loose. She pulled back her shoulders and, in a rage, said, "You heard the man, jack off for us, you f**king worthless piece of s**t, just like you did that day when you followed me."

His friends quickly spoke up, "Man, we don't want any problems."

I told them to get out of here and then pointed at the one that victimized her. "If I ever see you again, I am going to fix it so that you won't ever walk again."

I could feel my best friend's relief. She was smiling, relieved, and back to herself. The empowerment of a woman was in the air; you could cut it with a knife.

Together, we moved to Eagle Heights, a neighborhood on the UW campus. We were teammates. I was working two jobs, had just graduated from the police academy, and was finishing my master's degree.

One day, my woman came with bad news. She had to go back to the islands to get her school/work visa requirements met. We cried a little bit, but at the same time there was excitement for her because she was going to be able to see her family. She promised she would be right back after she met her requirements.

Then I met my daughter Joshlynn's mother. Have you ever done something wrong and you knew it was wrong while you were doing it, but the result was both sad and beautiful at the same time? A lot of guilt can come from those decisions.

Joshlynn's mother contacted me saying we needed to talk. As our food was placed before us, she took her first bite.

I asked, "What do you need to talk to me about?" I was thinking it could be, "I want to quit talking to you" or "I really like you and we should be a couple." It could have gone either way.

She stood up quickly, ran to the nearest garbage can and puked. She wiped the puke off her mouth, sat back down, and said with a crackly voice, "I am pregnant and it's yours!"

I took a deep breath. My mind was racing. I started to stutter and sweat. But I knew what I had to do. Man up. Cowboy up, or whatever you want to call it. I remember saying, "If you are pregnant with my baby, I hope you plan on keeping the child." Thank God she did and shared the same thought.

I think this is a critical part of this book for my young readers to learn from. The choices you make sometimes can affect you the rest of your life. Sometimes great outcomes can come carrying a path of guilt, stress, depression, and many other emotions. I will let my readers decide what they thought I learned at this moment and maybe even think of what you would have done or how you would have handled the situation.

Joshlynn's mother is an educated, strong-minded Black woman who had two other children. Her pregnancy was not pretty. She was very ill, and I started going to her house often to help. I'd pick up the kids from daycare and take care of them until she got home from work. I would stay to assist. I helped potty-train her daughter. The kids really started to grow on me. I love them!

I don't think I missed a single doctor check-up. I enjoyed watching the amazing growth of life on the ultrasound machines. Still too early to identify gender, I couldn't help my dreams for what this baby boy was going to look like. I even said I was going to name him Joshua because I wanted to watch him squash all those football dreams I hadn't been able to achieve. I was going to teach him to love nature, school, and how to be a man!

Then I started to worry that he would have a heart condition like mine and asked the doctor to look into it, to keep an eye on it. I wouldn't want a child to be born with that because it is quite the struggle. It really bothered me that this was a possibility.

After waiting for what seemed like years, the excitement of being able to identify the gender was on us! In a dark room, they lubricated her belly with the jelly for ultrasounds. The nurse moved the wand around. I watched in suspense. There was the baby. She looked at me and said, "Are you guys ready to know the gender of your baby?"

"Yaaaaaaaas!"

She looked right at me and said, "Daddy, your family is going to welcome a newwwwwww baby girl!"

Well, that changed things drastically in my head! I was tremendously excited and just wanted her to be healthy but at the same time, I had a Karma thought that still haunts me. They say Karma is a bitch and for the remaining months of the pregnancy, I tossed and turned. My God, I had met her mother at a stoplight while living with another woman. How about all the women I played and hurt? What about those real nasty conversations I have been a part of in locker rooms, bars, and just hanging out.

Oh, man, I am f**ked, I thought. But I can't say I wasn't warned. Boys will be boys, right? A daughter, a real daughter.

The day finally arrived. We traveled to Meriter Hospital at 4am for the planned C-section. It was dark as we drove, and I remember she looked at me with a smile. "Are you ready for this?" I said yes but I was nervous.

The anticipation. The excitement. This was the day. We entered the birthing room and this beautiful process started. They prepared the sterilization and gave her the proper medications. The doctor entered. I was seated back by Joshlynn's mother's head.

The baby came out looking very much like me but a perfect combination of both her mother and me. Light, soft skin that smelled so fresh. Dark, silky, curly hair. A timid cry.

Suddenly, my life changed. I fell in love. It was a different kind of love, an unexplainable love. Mine to enjoy and protect! Oh, my God, I am a dad or a daddy, as she now calls me.

We chose to keep her by us for the night instead of sending her to the nursery. We positioned the hospital baby bed right between us. We held her hands as she slept and every time she woke up, we would pass her back and forth to caress her.

My mother was already there to help us out and brought the other two children to the hospital to see her. They were so happy and took turns holding her.

We brought this little Black Queen home. Everyone fell in love with her the minute they saw her. She had a full head of those curls and big eyes that studied you. When I brought her to work, she stared at my co-worker, Jerome, as he held her. He said, "Brother, what a blessing. She is going to be smart. Look how she is looking in my eyes!"

Born on November 3rd, 2009, the best gift a man could have asked for was brought into this world. A gift. A joy. A purpose and a sure sign of a higher power.

HEART SURGERY, APRIL 2010—AM I GOING TO DIE?

In March 2010, following Joshlynn's birth, I had a stroke. The doctors told me I was healthy and to revisit them in five months.

A few weeks later, I was finishing a writing assignment for my master's degree course work. I felt tired and like I needed to burp. The heavy feeling in my chest would not pass and it got worse.

My maw was ironing clothes and I told her I wasn't feeling the best, like I had gas. I was asking if she had anything to relieve it when suddenly the pressure got worse. I bent over and grabbed my chest.

Maw yelled, "Call 911."

I caught my breath on the porch, waiting for the ambulance. The cold air assisted my breathing and had a natural calming effect. I could hear the sirens in the distance and remember thinking, "My God, my God, not now, please, please don't take me now. I just got this beautiful gift. My daughter. God, please, I had thought I was dumb my entire life and I am getting a masters' degree. God, not now. I love my life. I will be a better man. Promise."

I had tears in my eyes as the ambulance pulled up. One of the paramedics said, "You are in good hands now."

"Sir, I am scared, I have aortic valve stenosis, and I took an aspirin this morning, just in case I went lights out. Here comes that chest weight again!"

"What are you feeling?" the paramedic asked.

"Man, not good." I began feeling tense, sweaty, and like I might pass out.

"Hold on, big man. We are almost there." He turned and told the driver, "Faster. Hit the siren."

Nurses and physicians met us at the emergency room doors. Moving fast! As the paramedics and hospital staff shared information, I began autogenic breath, which I had been taught in a defense class at the Department of Corrections. Breathe in through the nose for four seconds, hold for four, and exhale slowly for four. Repeat. It slows the heart rate in serious situations and could save your life if you get shot or stabbed.

Oxygen and morphine were added. I relaxed.

After many questions and much monitoring, the cardiologist came into my room alone. He was a tall older gentleman, probably toward the end of his career. He asked if I minded if he sat for a minute so we could talk, then asked about my life and heart history. He gracefully moved into father mode, putting his hand on mine, and said, "I am sorry to tell you, but your aortic valve has run its course. It is worn out and needs to be removed. I must be honest with you we are not in the best of situations. Remember when they told you to come back in five months at the other hospital? My professional opinion is we don't have that kind of time."

With tears in my eyes, I said, "I am a new father and I have to be here!"

I looked at him directly, man to man. He kind of held his head low and I couldn't see his eyes.

Eye contact is a silent way of speaking, of communicating. I was taught young to look a man in his eyes when talking. The streets taught me you can tell a lot about a man by his eye contact. It develops a strong human bond because your eyes are taking pictures. You and the other person will forever be in that photo together and only the two of you will be able to see it.

"Can I ask you something, sir?" I said in a weak voice.

He raised his head and this was when the photos from our eye-contact moment began. He had tears running down his cheeks as his eyes slowly met mine.

"Am I going to die?"

He apologized for the tears, wiping them from under his glasses. He explained, "I feel that we might have caught this at a perfect time. More tests need to be done but one thing is certain, you are going to need a transplant of the valve sleeve, and then possibly a pacemaker."

I leaned to the edge of the bed so I could get closer to him, his tears already answered my question. In desperation, I pleadingly said, "Not only am I a new father, but I also am a student. I work with guys getting out of prison who need me."

I am not sure where all of that came from, but I told him, "I only ask one favor of you. Don't treat me as a patient. Treat me as your brother or son, pay great attention to every detail, and demand that of everyone who works with you."

He promised.

If I followed protocol, they said, I could go home for a week or two and prepare for the transplant. I had to take off work. And tell my friends and family. The direct orders were, "Go home, take it very easy, don't lift anything, and call 911 if you have an emergency."

Did I want a bovine, swine, or a mechanical heart valve? Arnold Schwarzenegger had a tissue pulmonary valve that I believe was grown from his own muscle. His kind of valve surgery wasn't offered to me. I can probably guess why. Comedian Robin Williams and "The Voice" of the Milwaukee Brewers had valve replacement surgeries around the same time I did.

I chose the mechanical valve because it lasted the longest and was less likely to have to be replaced. The downfall was I would have to be on blood thinners and other medications the rest of my life. Blood thinners are dangerous and require constant monitoring. If your blood is too thin you can bleed to death from even a minor head injury. Too thick and it can stick to the mechanical valve, causing a stroke.

* * *

My surgeon was a handsome man from another country with a cool name and accent. I could smell his confidence and was feeding off it, feeling more comfortable. He had a certain kind of swagger—an arrogance like a military fighter pilot, a demeanor needed to hold such a position.

In football terms, he was Tom Brady. Although I haven't been a Tom Brady fan, I can appreciate his game intelligence, his drive for success, and his leadership on the field. If I were in Vegas, I'd be betting on Brady every time.

The doctor also said that, after the surgery, I wouldn't be able to drink alcohol anymore, ride motorcycles, participate in contact sports, or do anything that could cause bleeding.

What he didn't say was, "Prepare yourself for what will be going through in your head as we wait for your big game day in a few weeks."

My surgery.

While waiting for my big game, my thoughts were all over the place. I briefly considered taking my own life. I was so pissed off. I thought about getting a gun, a case of beer, sneaking into Madison's Camp Randall Stadium, and blowing my heart out my back on the

50-yard line. I thought about going back home and doing it on the football field we played on growing up, but that felt disrespectful to everyone who knows me and loves me, and disrespectful to the field that taught me so much.

Selfish thoughts these were!

I hadn't learned to quit on that football field. I learned to never give up. I learned to vanquish and rise to the occasion. To believe in myself and my teammates. To listen to our coaches. To work harder than our opponents. To think about team before self, and to give 'er hell!

While all this was crossing my mind, I was drinking a six-pack of Miller. I slammed down the last beer and called my high school coach to let him know what was going on. I needed to hear Coach H's voice— his non-coddling voice that demanded respect and made you feel like you were someone. After all, he and his Hall of Fame coaching staff taught me to think like this. I owe them my life for loving me, treating me with respect, and understanding that I was different on the inside. The day I picked up that football and started talking to it, I joined a fraternity—a fraternity of men led by Coach H!

FOOTBALL FLASHBACK—
"ARE YOU COLD, CLAUER?"

When Coach H came to town, the Lancaster Flying Arrows were struggling. He instantly surrounded himself with other coaches who carried his same philosophies and caring ways. Later, they all ended up in the Wisconsin Football Coaches Hall of Fame. Each of them played a valuable part in my story.

I think I was in the 7th grade when I first met Coach H. Not real sure. He was a short, stocky man with a big bark. He drove a little red car with UW–River Falls stickers on it. It was beat-up and likely the car he drove in college. It always had footballs in it. Coaching the Flying Arrows may have been his first job out of college. He stayed and started his family in town.

Coach knew the story about my heart and not being able to play contact sports. He even knew my only option was to be a punter and kicker.

One summer day, I was walking to a field to practice my punting when that beat-up red car, with its loud muffler, pulled up next to me. Coach H asked if I needed a ride. I was reluctant to accept because I had a mouth full of chewing tobacco and knew that was against the athletic code. But I accepted the ride and instantly saw him hide a bag of Redman Plug in the center console. Maybe it was good that I had that tobacco in my mouth because it gave me an opportunity to keep my mouth shut and listen. I couldn't wait to get to the field though. For starters, I didn't want to get in trouble and secondly, I was gagging on that s**t with a mouthful of spit.

That ride, that moment in time, was life-changing. He said things on that short ride like, "I am watching you. Work hard. There are camps for punters and kickers that I will look into." Most importantly, he showed compassion. He explained that punters and kickers are not well liked in the sport, but they are a necessity. He explained that "special teams" are the third phase of football and are equally as important as the other two.

As we pulled up to the high school, a bunch of older dudes were waiting outside for him to open the weight room. He gave them all love while he was opening the door. I was practicing on the field as they began lifting and I could hear them laughing, yelling, and playing real loud pump-up music.

Occasionally, one would step outside with his shirt off to catch a cool breeze. Coach must have told some of them about me because they knew my name and were real encouraging. I know now what he was doing. He was including me to help me grow and give me a fighting chance. I wasn't the kid with the heart problem when I was around him; I was an athlete in training. If he considered punters and kickers athletes, then so did I.

Coach H looked at me standing there with my teammates, trying to stay warm. In front of the high school upperclassmen and in a loud voice, he said, "Clauer, are you cold"?

I respected him so I wasn't going to lie. "Yes, Coach, I am cold." Stupidest thing I ever said; I should have lied. He pointed at a grove of pine trees a few blocks away and said, "Go warm yourself up and get me a pinecone." This was his way of showing the team he wasn't going to baby me even though it might have looked like he was giving me this opportunity to be the team's kicker/punter at a young age. Some of the older guys snickered and were quickly redirected by their captains to shut the f**k up so they wouldn't have to get a pinecone.

If you pissed Coach H off during practice, you were sent to get a pinecone.

But the team knew that there was a knoll between the pine tree and where the coach couldn't see. The guys would stockpile pinecones for each other at the knoll, so no one had to go too far.

Yes, a fraternity of men, cleverly constructed by Coach H.

HEART SURGERY, APRIL OF 2010—
A REAL WALTER PAYTON JERSEY

I prepared for the heart surgery like it was a playoff game. The biggest playoff game of my life. My mental preparation flashed me back to football memories—images of those big games I had contributed to. And, with my ADHD, surgery and football mingled—important memories sailed through my brain. I was making connections between critical life events in ways that not everyone would, but it was working for me.

This kind of reframing—putting yourself in a safe bubble of your own creation—may be a strategy you want to try out when you are in a really bad spot. Substitute safer experiences for one that is incomprehensible.

Preparing for the big game, I got proper rest, meditated, and had long talks with God. But in case something went south, I didn't let Joshlynn out of my sight. If I died, I was going to go down fighting, but I sure was not losing any time with my baby.

A few days before the playoff game, I bought a Walter Payton jersey to wear on my game day. A real one! I was still having those negative thoughts so to block them, I would think of life like it was fourth and long, and my team needed a big punt. They needed me. Thinking like this, the negative thoughts dissipated.

I had this.

I didn't sleep much the night before the surgery, uh, the game. I ran the plays through my head. If this happens, I go here. If that happens, I go there. I did this like I was studying the opponent's film. I was looking for weaknesses and places I might be able to punt the ball to give us the best advantage.

I showered with their special antibacterial soap that morning and actually put my jersey on over a dress shirt and tie. Dress shoes and comfortable dress socks.

I got on the bus, took my seat by the window and mentally prepared. Kickoff was at 5:30 am. As the bus got closer to the stadium, I began looking out the window to check what the day's weather conditions were going to be. I was hoping that, if there was a wind, it was going to be a heaven's north to direct south. Punters hate wind but if it was going to blow, I wanted the wind to keep the ball down on the field.

WALKING THE LINE: THERE IS NO TIME FOR HATE

The stadium was all lit up and the (med-flight) helicopters were already coming and going, probably shooting-game day videos for the news, I imagined, 'cause this was the big one. If we won, we were going to the Super Bowl with an opportunity of being champions of the world!

I checked in with stadium security and they pointed me to the away-team locker room, to start prepping for my 10:30 game.

This was personal to me. This was the match that beat my grandpaw on October 26th, 1967. My grandmaw played and lost on November 8th, 1996. My uncle wears a heart surgery scar from his playoff game in the 1990s.

Mentally preparing for this surgery that could take my life, I flashed back to my first high school football experiences.

FOOTBALL FLASHBACK—
FRESHMAN YEAR OF HIGH SCHOOL

Finally, we were Flying Arrows with big shoes to fill after the class ahead of us had an undefeated season. As freshmen, what we lacked in size, we made up for with speed and heart.

I practiced punting over kicking. I loved the thought of hanging a ball up in the air so a gutsy returner might refuse the fair catch and get lit up by our crew, changing the tone of the game. I was part of this four-quarter chess match. In the fight.

The guys voted me to represent them on the homecoming court. A kicker/punter on the court! They can never understand what that meant to me. Being included and accepted was something I had been starving for my whole life. Now I was part of a crew who enjoyed sitting quietly together on long bus rides, just to get off and whoop ass. We would bleed for the Flying Arrows yellow and royal blue.

HEART SURGERY, APRIL OF 2010—
MENTAL PREPARATION

Not a lot of people get the opportunity to play in big games like this, to bleed for the team.

I remember my high school coach standing before us prior to a big playoff game preparing us mentally. He would say things like:

> "Today is your day, your day, do you know what that means, fellas? It means that if you believe in yourself, have prepared properly and have just enough dog in you, you will live to see another one; the season will continue. Today is not the day to give up, today is not the day to go hide under a rock, today is the day to take the field and let your opponent know this is your mother-f**king backyard, and you make the rules up in here. Four quarters. That's what I need out of you. Four quarters of punch them in the mouth football. We are going to keep our foot on the gas from the first tick on the clock until the fat lady sings. Let's get this s**t."

I have never liked playing at the UW Hospitals and Clinics stadium. Gloomy. And the crowd can get nasty. My family was coming to town: my parents, Joshlynn's mom, and my cousin Brian were already there. Linda Ketchum, my boss, was on her way and so were Barbara and Everett, my co-workers.

All said they were sending prayers.

Security was tight. A lot of silence in the locker room with my parents and cousin Brian. I think they didn't want to make me nervous. Outcomes of games like this, whether you win or lose, will change your life and the lives of those around you forever.

Dad said, "Good luck."

Maw said, "Go get 'em, kid."

Brian hugged me, smiled, and said he'd see me after the game.

Then one of the team managers came and said that the coaches wanted me in the locker room to start taping. I had my own personal table with my name on it. The trainer asked me to remove all my clothing. She shaved my chest hair and wiped me down. Blood pressure, pulse, and oxygen level monitors were set up.

Having my headphones on calmed me. I flashed back to my sophomore football year. We won the conference that year and made it a few games into the playoffs.

FOOTBALL FLASHBACK— SOPHOMORE YEAR OF HIGH SCHOOL

At this point, I would say the relationship with Coach H was simply love. Would he move some of us up from the JV team to Varsity, to make names for ourselves and start this s**t early?

"Clauer. Suit up for special teams. Varsity. If you get playing time, you earned it." Coach meant that. We knew this was a privilege. Relax. Relax.

I entered the huddle with the play, "Punt the ball." Man, could that senior snap the ball, fast, and on the money. It enabled me to get off some good balls. Maw, Dad, Grandmaw, Grandmaw, and Grandpaw, cousins, uncles, and aunties were there. I did it. Everyone, I did it!

I must tell you guys who are reading that this is the most emotional I have been while writing this book—these football memories merging with the surgery.

So much can be said about these times in my life. I know each of us can have this feeling. We just need to have the right people at the right times. I am football-pumped as I write this, but am also feeling appreciation, gratitude, love, and friendship.

And for some reason, I am crying.

I will do my best to keep it real and explain these emotions, but you don't get these all the time in life, so it is hard to explain.

That Friday night, under the Varsity team lights, my life changed forever, and it was because a group of coaches got together with my positive friends and decided to encourage and challenge me to be great. I was no longer feeling dumb. My shoulders were back, and my head held high. I was not the kid with the heart problem.

That night I became Joshua Clauer, #88, the Punter.

I will never forget that moment in time. That night, those weird conversations I'd had with all those footballs started to make sense. It had worked.

I wore my first tie that year. I learned from Coach L, "If you look good, you look good; if you feel good, you feel good; if you play good, you win." (Thanks, Coach/RIP.)

My statistics got me Predicted for the Pre-Season All Area Team for the next season. We were bringing the game back to Lancaster. We were making a name for ourselves, but little did we know we were creating a football giant in the state of Wisconsin. We were creating what they call in sports a dynasty. Lancaster had had very few consistent winning seasons, but after our group graduated, state championship after state championship became a tradition.

We were building something special even though we did not go to state during my years.

HEART SURGERY, APRIL OF 2010—
THOU ANOINTEST MY HEAD WITH OIL

Thirty minutes until surgery kickoff. They moved me to a room closer to the field. A couple of coaches came in to go over details before the game. I even signed a few things in case something bad happened. It's a rough sport.

I am different than a lot of the athletes. The Catholic priest travels with me. He came in and asked if I was ready and before leaving, he put his hand on my head saying, *"Yea though I walk through the valley of the shadow of death, I will fear no evil: for thou art with me; Thy rod and thy staff they comfort me. Thou preparest a table before me in the presence of mine enemies: Thou anointest my head with oil; my cup runneth over."*

Then my priest walked away.

Just like the University of Notre Dame Fighting Irish, there is a priest in the room. My thoughts returned to my junior year in football.

FOOTBALL FLASHBACK— JUNIOR YEAR OF HIGH SCHOOL

By our junior season, we were battle-ready, dressing in that old, grimy, dirty locker room that produced a blue-collar feel. That was exactly what we were.

As we lined up to slowly walk to the field, you could hear guys breathing heavy, snorting, and some even punching s**t on the way out the door. Walking to the field like boxers to the ring. "Let's go, Arrows. Go—Fight—Win."

The media was there, pregame talk on the radio. Fight night. Excitement was in the air in a part of the world where there is not much to get excited about and we were the main attraction. Put on a show because so many were watching and living vicariously. I puked before every game and that was my sign that I was ready.

The special-education kids wore their blue and gold. They yelled our names. Always give them a hug or a high five before the game because they were our biggest fans.

For those who are not at the game because of older age, they were at home with the radio on. They didn't even know the sport but just want to hear their family or friend's name called over the radio.

Our cheerleaders would get the crowd going with a chant, "All the way to state, all the way to state, get your ticket now, get your ticket right now."

At that time, Reggie Roby was one of the only Black punters in the NFL and had an average punt of 45.7 yards. I punted similarly. The radio announcer started calling me Reggie Roby. Some guys back home still call me Reggie or Reg. Total respect. Sweet. I went from a little boy who loved Walter Payton to loving guys like Reggie Roby? Unbelievable.

HEART SURGERY, APRIL OF 2010—
THE SOUND OF LIFE!

In the operating room, the anesthesiologist said, "You are going to be okay." As he injected me, he said, "Good luck and when you wake up, I'll probably be at my vacation destination."

I woke up several hours later, highly sedated with a tube shoved down my throat and two tubes sticking out the side of my belly. I couldn't talk and was very swollen.

Brian and my other cousin, Ryan, were there. I saw their backs as they were leaving. My dad was heading out as well but was looking back at me. He looked tired and scared.

I tried to talk as he walked away. I was trying to yell, "Dad, help me."

I couldn't get it out, so I started to tug on the tube gagging my throat. I figured if I ripped this tube out, he could hear me. He didn't and someone I couldn't see stopped me.

I slept for about a day but was constantly interrupted by hospital staff. When I was finally up, my maw said that my MUM co-workers stayed the entire time. They were praying for me; wasn't that kind of them.

All I know is that I felt like I actually got hit by a dump truck. My sternum area hurt even if I moved a little bit. I sneezed once and it felt like I got a shotgun blast in the chest. I didn't want to move, and I sure didn't want to sneeze again. The nurse said they were going to take me for a walk as soon as they took the tube out of my throat.

It was a young nurse from my hometown who took me for my first walk of probably less than 50 feet. He was younger than me, but he played football for the Arrows. He knew of me. He was my post-surgery cheerleader. He knew just what to say.

I was alive but what was this loud ticking in my ears? It sounded to me like someone was in the room and beating on a drum. A sharp sound. So abnormal.

It was driving me nuts and it wouldn't go away.

Tick tick tick tick.

What the f**k was that?

Apparently, it was the sound of life!

It was the titanium parts of my valve hitting and I could hear it. I didn't know if I would get used to this, but I did.

Game over.

FOOTBALL FLASHBACK—
SENIOR YEAR OF HIGH SCHOOL

Senior year, we did not win the conference. In gym class, I broke my jaw in two places. It had to be wired shut and I went from 170 to 130 pounds, drinking through a straw for a month.

Back then, punters and kickers were not being looked at for scholarships, were not being appreciated. I was peaking just before the jaw accident, getting those stat numbers up. I had to sit out one game because the wire would present a lot of danger.

Coach and I took my mouthpiece and carved out the inside so it looked like I had a mouthguard. I teed up a ball for a kickoff and the referee asked how I was feeling, then winked at me. He knew what we were doing.

Yep, game over.

THE TICK OF LIFE AND JOSHLYNN

As I became accustomed to the new acoustics playing in my head, I began to realize that it was the sound of life. My life. Although it was annoying, I got used to it.

It presented embarrassments in quiet rooms. I remember one time I was conducting a group. It was quiet. A client said, "What the f**k is that ticking?" I explained that it was me and he said, "Man, that must be an expensive watch."

"No, it's just me!"

(What he didn't know was that Rolex watches don't tick.)

In my head, the heart valve beat like a native drum where peace and love pounded through my veins. I could picture Native American elders sitting around a powwow drum, singing an earthly song just for me. Other times, I could imagine a young historically Black college drum line entertaining a crowd letting them feel their heartbeat through magnificent rhythms of life.

As I healed like a newborn, my own baby was growing right beside me. Joshlynn began to use my heart tick as a nurturing rhythm to fall asleep. She could fall asleep quickly with her ear against her daddy. As she slept, it was a magnificent feeling of two hearts truly joining as one, both vulnerable and weak.

Fathers are supposed to be strong physically and mentally. My baby was born during one of the weakest points in my life. Even I was wetting myself often during this time; it wasn't just her. But she was giving me the energy I needed to grow. Our commingled heartbeats meant something powerful.

As I recovered, she grew. We would exercise her legs and got her a jumping swing that we hung in the kitchen. She could jump all day and even jump herself to sleep. This is how she earned the nickname "Jump -Jump"!

Looking into Joshlynn's eyes, I could feel a higher power. I could feel my responsibility as a man. Before my surgery I had a few football news articles about me imbedded into wood plaques in case I passed away. The idea was that the articles would give her some good leads on the type of man her daddy was and what was important to him during parts of his life.

Now I was so blessed to have this opportunity to spend more time with her in this life. I thanked God. I prayed for better opportunities for her and an easier life than I have had.

My co-workers at MUM were so generous that they made sure I was still getting paid during my time off. Although the doctor said I needed to take it easy, I started back to work early coaching a semi-pro team. Man, I love the game of football and what it does for people.

Have you figured that out? It is an unexplainable love.

But if you really want to talk about an unexplainable love, there is the love I have for my daughter. It is love at an entirely new level. And combine my two loves, well, what can I say!

Joshlynn was on the football sidelines before she could talk. She was in a stroller right behind me.

I was so weak when I joined the semi-pro coaching staff, I could barely get around. Joshlynn's mom packed us all up in her van and drove us to the first practice so that I could introduce myself.

I stood before them, cold and weak. I looked at my audience, a lot of Black faces and some tough-looking White boys who I am sure had a story surrounded by poverty. They all came from the ghettos of Milwaukee, Kenosha, and Racine. I could see it in their eyes that they didn't care if this was Division 1 football or the NFL. They were playing because they loved the game for what it had done for them at some point in their lives!

"Good morning, yawl! My name is Coach Clauer and I will be the special team's coach for the season. I must apologize if you can't hear me 'cause my voice is a little weak and I stutter sometimes. My family is sitting over there in the car with my newborn daughter. I recently had heart surgery and just wanted to come down here to introduce myself to you fellas. I see it in yawl eyes that each and every one of you are hungry. This game has been good to me. Some of you are old enough to understand what I am saying and some of you are young enough to learn from what I am saying.

"This game saved my life. It gave me choices, friendships, and a fraternity that I am proud to be a part of. I've been to a few cookouts, I am not new to this game and could have been an NFL player. If you want to utilize this game for friendships, that's great. If you want to utilize it to keep you out of trouble, that's great too. But if you want to utilize this game to get noticed by colleges or the NFL, we need to set an example both on and off the field.

"Make smart choices when you are not here and as far as practice goes, work your hardest. How hard we practice dictates the level of ass whooping's we will hand out this year. We can hand out playground ass whoopings or we can lay out you-robbed-my-momma ass-whoopings. I will tell yawl one thing. I am a team player. I love this game and I can't wait to share my love with yawl dogs."

They clapped and cheered. I went home.

GANG RESPONSE INTERVENTION TEAM

One morning, when I was back working at MUM, I heard a deep, strong voice say, "Hey, Josh, come here." It was John, whose office was right next to mine. We did a lot of hollering back and forth in the office. Teammate!

I went to his office. He said his best friend just called him and said that there was a Gang Response Intervention Team job opening. I didn't know what it was or consisted of, but he said, "Look, mate, I've been watching you around these kids and you love it. I love it too, but I am coming to the end of my career. I think you should apply for it, but you only have tonight to fill out the application because I am late seeing it."

"But I love MUM, John. Do you think I have a chance? They might want someone Black or Brown."

"They need you and you will do great; just don't forget about me. We got this here. Go change lives out of love and compassion and you will be rewarded, plus, it's more fun working with you. Those kids will have a fighting chance."

I spent the entire night applying for that job. A week later, I was interviewed and got it! I have not looked back.

Almost ten years have passed since John did me a solid and told me to apply for that job. The work with gang interventions is non-stop trauma. Non-stop trauma. I work with high school youth, poor kids coming up in adverse situations who need extra opportunities because of all the barriers they face. They are at a crossroads. These young men and women are victims of a vicious world that creates cycles of nonstop confusion, loss, heartache, and tears. Their struggles are real. There are successes and failures. We lose a lot of people to the streets, and to death.

Working with juveniles again after a long stretch of working with adults was exciting but very different because they are so young and there is still innocence to preserve. This job isn't for everybody. It requires persistence, resilience, mental strength, kindness, and truth.

* * *

Although this is a government position (Dane County, Madison, Wisconsin), we are in the trenches and I work with some of the most caring and compassionate human beings on the planet who sacrifice themselves for others.

This might sound crazy, but you know how when a police officer, prison guard, or a firefighter passes away, they are respected and honored. These folks I work with deserve that too—an honor burial when they die. They hold titles like Social Worker, Program Leader, Reentry Specialist, or Social Services Specialist; they are deserving of battle honors and war cries. Trench workers! F**king angels! I like to think that when trench workers enter the next life, they sit around the table with other soldiers like them and with those who will live in infamy like Malcolm and Martin. Imagine the greeting and hospitality that would occur. It would rap something like this:

As she entered, Martin opened the door
Huey P. Newton was reading
And Malcolm was facing Mecca on the floor

"Where am I?" she asked as she entered the room
Then an old sounding voice sounded
Well, it's not the moon.

It was Harriet Tubman who was sitting in the back
Next to a boxing champ who said his name was Jack.

As the table filled and the meals were placed
Bob said that the fruit was from Jamaica,
"You will love how it taste."

Crazy Horse led everyone in prayer and
was addressed as Sir
I'm sorry you didn't know where you were.

"Why am I here?" she asked,
Just as the fruit and spliff was passed
"We have to confess we have been watching your life,"
Mandela said
We are honored to have you with us, over there is your bed.

"But I didn't do nothing great with my life
I wasn't even a good mother or a wife."

Walter stood up with his man-of-the-year-honor
"Can I speak, hope it's not a bother."

"You did your time in those streets, Sis
How many personal celebrations did you miss?"

"I remember when your son turned five
You were at a hotel getting a family a room to stay
To keep them safe and alive.

That one kid that died from that stray bullet
He is right over there sitting by that poet.

Maya, she thought was her name but wasn't quite sure
So many people, it was such a blur.

The guy sitting to her right, he was hard to explain
The back of his jersey read Aaron
I just assumed it was his name.

He said, "Read what we put on that note
Latasha Harlins proofed it
We thought you should know."

The note read such a beautiful story about a life well-lived
Emmitt Till clapped and
Gave a grin.

As she started to read she couldn't believe all that they
thought was so great
But it was those late nights laying restless
that she learned to hate.

She shed many tears throughout her career
Those deep dark stories
She will always hold dear.

So much sadness she had to see
And people around her saying
At least it wasn't me.

Fear for your own family was constantly on your mind
Because you are the one who knows the world
Isn't kind.

Child victims of the worst s**t that life has to offer
Another teenage client called
About to have a daughter.

You spent countless hours under stress with
a disheveled mind
You even tried to drink it away one time.

But that didn't work too good for you, did it
It was a disaster, the New Jim Crow
We were glad you read it.

The last paragraph is what hit her the most
What they had to say about her deserved a toast.

They used words like thank you, sister and love you much
For being a soldier of fortune with a human touch.

As she got to the last line, they began the toast
It was your spirit that we loved, that we loved
The Most!
                          —Joshua Clauer

GANGS IN A LITTLE CITY—
TWO WORLDS COLLIDE

Covid-19 has given me time to step away and self-reflect. I realized I've had experiences not many people have. I use the combination of my education and experiences to try to help others. But at times, I have a hard time coping with what I see (and know).

One time, when my daughter was still in a car seat, I pulled into a PDQ gas station. Some dope addicts were hanging outside. I held my daughter's hand as we walked in; she was all dolled up. When we came out, one guy said, "Your daughter's really hot." I opened her door and buckled her in her car seat. Then I turned to the guy and said, "What did you just say to me about my daughter?"

"I said she is hot."

I retorted, "You might want to rephrase that."

He said, "No, you heard exactly how I said it."

My daughter felt the animal, the vibrations, in me so much, she pleaded, "Don't kill him, Daddy."

At the same time, she knows my love and tenderness. I always walk a line.

I remember, when I was young, my father and his friends talked about the African American man who was running for the mayor of Madison. He was trying to tell the city to prepare for the future, both for the city's sake and to help his people that he knew were coming.

Some people gave him the nickname "Crazy."

This man was not crazy. He was worried. He was paying attention to what was going on in Chicago's warzones: some of the harshest neighborhoods, housing projects, and urban wars in the country. Crazy realized the neglect many of these soon-to-be migrants to Madison had endured; their struggles and the untreated post-traumatic stress that filled in their backpacks.

What would you do if your kids and your family were in danger? Would you want to raise a child in a warzone? Would you have the courage to uproot your life and escape? To migrate?

Obviously not all migrants from Chicago come with backpacks full of troubles, but too many were coming to escape the marked territories, where going to school could mean walking through rival gang neigh-

113

borhoods. One father told me about daily walking his child to school through gang members selling crack, prostitutes selling their bodies for more crack, and unfortunately even a few dead bodies that hadn't been discovered yet.

What was the Chicago history causing this migration?

Many families had migrated from the South during the Black Migration between 1916 and 1970, to seek opportunities away from racial segregation. Now they were migrating again, this time under 200 miles.

The Chicago Housing Authority has had a big hand in Madison's situation. In the mid-1930s there was a bright idea of stacking economically poor people in public housing projects. The last of these Chicago projects was razed in 2011. As the projects tumbled, thousands of people were removed, and hyper-gentrification bloomed at its best.

Have you ever been in, or seen a video of, a crowd when shots were fired? Everyone runs to safety. This is what happened when gentrification started in Chicago. People ran to safety and opportunity. One of those locations was Madison, Wisconsin.

Madison was safe. There were jobs and housing that was affordable even without public assistance. People came packed in busses and cars, excited for a new opportunity. I remember when a grandmother, her daughter, and all the grandchildren were found concealed under a blanket in downtown Madison. They had just arrived. The woman said something like, "I would rather be cold and homeless under a blanket in Madison, Wisconsin, than where we just came from."

I am friends with an old lady who lived on Chicago's westside. She moved to Madison because her son got incarcerated for selling crack and was going to go to prison. She said, "The boy was brought to Madison on weekends, to sell. He was making a lot of money. But nothing else. He didn't even know where to run. I miss him so."

Have you ever opened your door to a family member you loved but whose life was very different? I have. After about a day I wondered, What did I get myself into? Trauma, addiction, poverty, unemployment, and lack of mental health help. To take on a roommate like this takes consideration and proper resources. Planning, like Crazy was suggesting.

These Chicago folks were escaping war and moving in. They needed time to breathe in their newly found safe land. And the welcoming committee was all lined up.

Welcome to Madison where you and your family can enjoy our lakes, parks, and colleges if you are interested.

The only thing missing in the welcome basket was the right questions. "We know you need housing, employment, and to get your kids in schools. Aww they are so cute;" you know the intended kindness we so often hear from people who must smile for a living. And maybe someone does ask these questions, but they should be more persistent:

What have you witnessed?

What do you really need right now?

How much education and what job skills do you have?

What are your children's school needs?

How can we help you?

* * *

When my father got home from the Vietnam war, he went to college for a spell. He wanted to be an engineer but was so traumatized from war that he found himself struggling. He couldn't do it. I don't believe anyone asked him what he really needed or how he could have been helped.

Chicago is no different than Vietnam. Why do you think it earned the nickname *Chiraq*? Compare Chicago statistically to the Iraq War in terms of shootings and death. What do you see?

It's easy to hate when all you have witnessed is genocidal feuds and you have no one to trust. You can't even trust the people who look like you: your teachers, your bus drivers, your doctors, your mailman, even the local cops.

Do you know how many times in my career I have been told that I am the first White man someone ever took the time to know? For some, the only experience they ever had with White people was from television. (Much like many Whites who have never met an African American but have only seen them on TV.)

It's easy to skip school and flunk out when all that is in your mind is the memory of that kid that you used to ride big wheels with because you were riding together when he got hit by a bullet. You were left holding his head up and yelling for help while his legs were still stuck in the big wheel, twitching.

It is easy to give up when you are frightened or sad or feeling lost by the pressures of a new culture. It may be safer and prettier in Madison, but there is the stealth atmosphere of White privilege and White supremacy lurking around the edges that you cannot quite identify.

Madison residents get new neighbors who are feeling the pressures of a fresh society. This impacts ALL of us. To be welcomed is one thing, but it's not enough. To me, welcomed is a two-way feeling that is shared from the heart and is embraced with love. *Welcoming* to me is saying, "I got your back in my house and I hope you got mine."

* * *

Think about crack cocaine. I'm not sure who invented it in the '80s or '90s, but you can be sure it wasn't a couple of poor boys who wasted a bag of powder cocaine to see what happened if you cooked it, whipped it on the stove, and added baking soda.

What does this mean for Madison? When Crazy was running for mayor, a small rock of cocaine went for $5 in Chicago and $20 in Madison. This was a no-brainer business decision for these budding criminal enterprises. It is my opinion that whenever you mistreat anyone and do not offer them the same opportunity as everyone else or make the opportunity obtainable for all, you will have gangs. People gathered for safety and control, which is essentially what a gang is.

Gangs are not new and surely not to the City of Chicago where they have a sexy image. Gangland. Gang culture is embedded in the city's streets. Think of Al Capone during Prohibition, often leaving people in pools of blood for snitching or for going up against him in sales. He and his crew were the poster boys of Chicago gangs with beautifully tailored suits, money, and nice cars: the stuff of lore.

Gang life was where poor Italian kids could make it in the city of big shoulders. Idolized in martyrdom, people still discuss the blood battles and carnage witnessed in the Chicago streets. There are museums that house gang members' belongings. The buildings where they hung out or lived are venerated. I have met pregnant women who were thinking about naming their first son Capone.

Some people say there are no gangs in Madison. This normally comes from the mouth of someone who is basing their idea of gangs on what they have watched on TV or seen on a Chicago Gangster Tour. They haven't researched, haven't looked out the window, or haven't been in Madison's schools. No, it is not like Chicago and why would it be? The Iraq War is different than the Vietnam war, right? It's different playing football in Camp Randall than at your local high school field, isn't it? It is just a different location with different, but linked, problems.

Madison has gangs that are here or come in and out. Every race is represented. Many of the original Chicago gangs are present here with OGs (Original Gangster) who came during the Great Escape.

There is a lot of finger pointing that goes on around this topic and it seems like little progress is ever made. As the jobs left, crack came in, prisons were built, and the feds had a bright idea. Before and during the tear down of the Chicago housing projects, they decided to go in and cut off the head of the monster: the OG. The thinking was that if that were done, it would eradicate gangs and gang violence.

Cutting off the head meant they were going for the leaders, the CEOs of the gangs. What happened? The feds took the wheels off the wheelchair and people were stuck. The feds ran many gang sweeps and took founding members off the streets. These were the guys who called the shots, struck deals, and commanded orders. There was a chain of command and violations were handed out for breaking gang rules. That structure disappeared with the sweeps.

Consider what would happen if Aaron Rogers got hurt in pre-season and couldn't come back? Every quarterback from here to Georgia would be in competition for that spot, causing jealousy, infighting, and mass chaos.

Lack of gang leadership led to clique-banging. Splinters or factions developed everywhere like that rock that put a little crack in your car windshield. If you sleep on it, it will spider out like a fan and will cause you driving chaos. Cutting off the heads caused chaos in gangland.

* * *

For years, Madison's youth of color have feared going into very populated educational settings. If you ever want to see the face of segregation, just walk into a public-school cafeteria. Looks like a racing flag with two colors and only two squares.

Oh, but that is just where they like to sit, you know.

Da f**k you mean?

Maybe true to an extent, but why? Fear and lack of exposure.

And this is how a clique is formed. The following is my little story about just how a clique is formed in Madison, Wisconsin, among our juveniles.

Meet Bob.
Bob lives in Chicago.

Bob's father, Jake and all his brothers, joined the Dirty
Underwear Gang when they were around Bob's age.

Jake put in a lot of work for the Dirty Underwear Gang, sold
drugs, and maybe even caught a couple bodies. Not only was
Jake a member of the Dirty Underwear Gang but his dad was
also. Bob's daddy and granddaddy were legends in the
neighborhood and feared throughout the city.

Around the time Bob started to walk, Bob's dad got shot on
the South Side. By the time Bob could talk, his daddy was
gunned down on the front stoop of their one-bedroom flat on
a hot summer night while they were grilling hotdogs. They
were celebrating that his dad had gotten a new job and could
finally quit survival-mode work. This new employer wanted to
send him to school because they thought he was a great fit.

After Jake was shot on the stoop, Becky, Bob's mom, got
really depressed and started partying and smoking a lot of
weed. For a few weeks, Bob felt alone.
Then one night his granddaddy came over to talk to his
mother. The conversation was deep as Bob recalls. Bob says
he don't know why but he can't remember anything about the

night his daddy died. Apparently, he was the one who called 911. "It was like my brain closed, man," he said. Apparently from what granddaddy and Becky said in that conversation that night, their brain doors didn't close.

Grandaddy said he saw the car coming around the corner and someone got out. The driver was masked up. He went past and looked like he had gloves on. He said the dude in the car must have hated my daddy because Granddaddy explained that before the man shot, he took his mask off, gritted his teeth, and said, "Now what, bitch?" He also said that my daddy was gurgling blood out his mouth and nose. I guess it was a mess, but my momma said she was holding him when he died, and she could feel his heart beating when she started to help him. She said he was trying to say something, and she thought it was, "Loooooove you, Bobby, my boy... love you.

After that talk with my granddaddy, Mom and I moved to Madison. "I miss the city, dude. Miss my friends, more to do, and it's not so White, no offense. Can't wait for school to start and oh I forgot to tell you, my momma finally got an apartment, and my uncle Teddy is moving here to help out."

The school year started, and Becky got Bob some new shoes and a few outfits at Walmart. He loved the new outfits and the shoes, he felt, were banging. After all it was his first year of high school.

New apartment, new bus route, new school. New life.

His mom gave him a big kiss on the cheek, "I love you, baby, we are going to be okay, we will love it here. Make Momma proud, son." She closed the door.

As he stood out by the bus stop, Bob heard someone say, "Look at this fool shoes... this fool momma got his shoes at Walmart." Bob was too tough to show emotion plus he didn't want to f**k up this outfit that he still thought was on point.

When the bus got to the school, he started feeling sick and wanted to go home but he stood in line to be greeted by a big Black man with a shirt on that read, "Security." He scanned his new school ID, and he was off. "Make momma proud." He was there early because he got bussed and got to have breakfast before all the other students arrived.

His first class was decent he said but the teacher seemed racist. The second and third classes were a little better, but both of those teachers were old White ladies. Weird.

At lunch he wasn't sure where to sit as he was pulling a cheese sandwich out of his bag.

There were two cafeterias right next to each other. On one side there seemed to be a lot of quiet White kids, some Asians, a couple of African Americans, and people from other races.

You could choose which room you wanted to eat in, so he went to check out the other side before he made his decision. He said when he turned the corner, he couldn't believe it. The room was being monitored by police, school officials, social workers, janitors, and there were kids yelling, screaming, chasing each other. It smelled like straight skunk. As he sat nervously, scanning the room he heard a boy yell Pussy Foot Gang and another yelled Dirty Underwear. From another area someone yelled Jock Set.

After school, he had football practice. He seen a coach handing out granola bars to the players. He was starved but by the time he got to the box it was empty.

After practice he got on the bus and there was the boy who don't like his shoes. This time the bus wasn't just children. This time there were old ladies, regular people, and this time that boy had friends with him who looked older. The boy sat right by Bobby and said, "What it do bitch ass, let me get them shoes hoe, let me get them pants bitch." Bob tried to ignore this, but it was hard. The boy punched Bobby and his friends jumped in. They didn't take his shoes or pants, but they took his bus card.

Bobby didn't tell the bus driver and he sure didn't tell his mom because she couldn't afford another one. He had heard her say she couldn't afford it a million times before.

Daily, he kept pretending he was riding that bus to avoid getting in trouble with his mom. He made up excuses on why he was so late getting home from practice. For weeks he did this. He didn't have the heart to tell her that he was late for school every day and that he was lying about working out after practice. He got kicked off the team for being late for school and was now flunking first and second period and was falling asleep in all his other classes except gym. He thought he was going to pass gym class but didn't feel like changing his clothes and got docked points for that. Anyway, he didn't even have other clothes to change into.

One night while walking home from school, a car rolled up and it was the guys from the cafeteria who yelled Jock Set. They slowed up on him and asked if he needed a ride. They were all wearing hoodies that said Rest in Peace Jock Set Johnny and it had a picture of a boy on it. The picture was of a boy holding a gun in one hand and a few stacks in the other.

He got in the back of the car and told them he lived in the Elk Valley neighborhood, down on Rebecca Downs. They all laughed and each of them said they lived there when they first moved here too. One of them still did.

One boy said, "What set you claim?" Bob told them he didn't claim a set but that his dad had been a general for the DUs on the southside of Chicago. One boy jokingly said DUK

(Dirty Underwear Killa). He quickly stopped because he realized that's no way to greet a new friend and they all start explaining that Madison is different than Chicago. The only color we care about in Madison is green. He explained that his family all rolled with the DU. They wanted to become his friend on Facebook, and they laughed again when he pulled open his Obama phone.

The next day at school one of the boys gave him a smart phone that he had stolen last week at the mall across from the school. Bob now had access to Facebook. He became Facebook friends with the Jock Set boys he just met and some family and friends in Chicago. He even made his first post and his auntie hearted it and, in the comments, wrote, "Miss you baby boy can't wait to see you fam."

He was looking at some of the Jock Set pages. They were showing off guns, money, and talking nasty about females. They had Facebook names like Jock Set Stinky, Jock Set Itchy, and Jock Set Johnny. There were a lot of them and there were a lot of girls that were liking their stuff. He wanted more likes but just had his Auntie and a kid called Run Run, who wouldn't quit calling his phone.

He still carried his Obama phone that his momma gave him in case of an emergency. He shut his smart phone off at night and lied to his mom and told her he was making his post from the school computer.

About a week after having his phone, some guy named Pussy Foot Pauley JSK (Jock Set Killa) want to be his friend on the Book. Thinking the boy actually wanted to be his friend, he accepted the request. He also accepted because he heard you were considered a pussy if you didn't accept friend request from people that you are into it with.

Pussy Foot Pauley posted: "F**k that Walmart cloth wearing Bobby JS." Bobby couldn't figure out why he put the JS after his name. He wasn't Jock Set. PF Pauley continued with the post and even said he and the team ran a train on Bobby's momma, Becky. Bobby's auntie jumped on that post quick. "Watch your mouth little bitch," she said to Pussy Foot Pauley with a "You better get your boy Bobby."

It was right there that Bobby said he was forever challenged. His auntie meant that he needed to whoop that boy ass for saying that. Jock Set members started chiming in and one of them posted that tomorrow after school it was on and cracking and they were going to f**k up the Pussy Foots.

And it was at this point Bobby became Jock Set Bobby from the Brojects (he can't even use the letter P anymore).

* * *

Remember this clique (gang-to-be) with the messed-up name? They are all grown up now. A few of them are dead, a few of them in prison but now they are in deep. Not deep deep, but deep, getting close to deep deep! Deep starts when you start getting labeled as a gang member by law enforcement and community. Deep can be a slow walk or a fast run depending on circumstances. Deep Deep is when you raced so fast through the deep section that by the time you look for help, all that is left are one or two dudes with a ripped life vest and they are a block away.

JA CLAUER, MY SON,
AND THE NIGHT THAT FOREVER CHANGED ME

*I promise you that I will do heavenly work in honor of
your name. I will give myself to other little boys who look
like you and invest in their lives. I hope you hear me, son,
because Daddy keeps his promises.*

10/11/2013

My pregnant girlfriend went to the hospital earlier in the day because
she was very uncomfortable. Not feeling well. She was sent home to
rest and went to her auntie's house where she could be monitored
around loved ones.

I was working late but remained in phone contact with her. The
last time we spoke, she didn't sound well so I decided to drive to her
aunt's to check on her for myself.

A few weeks before, we found out she would be having a boy. She
already had a smart beautiful son, and I already had a smart beautiful
daughter. We probably both wanted the opposite of what the other
wanted to keep it real. She was probably thinking of hair bows, dresses,
and doing girl things because I was surely thinking of teaching a boy to
be a man.

When I found out the baby was a boy, man, I was overjoyed!

As I walked into her aunt's home on the southside, my girlfriend
was lying on the couch in the front room. She didn't look well, was
rocking back and forth, and looked scared. Her loved ones had looks of
worry and I said, "I want her to go back to the hospital."

In a fearful, panicky voice, my girlfriend chewed my ass. I knew it
was just her fear. Her auntie quickly settled her down and said, "I think
we should listen to the man and get you back to the hospital."

I left to go back to the office and punch out on the clock for the
night so I could be near her during this time.

Her auntie called saying they were on the way to the hospital. I
raced across the city.

When I got to her room, the doctor was just leaving and now
everyone looked scared. They told me that we were going to the labor
room where she would give birth to our son, early.

There was just one problem, and this is where my life changed forever. We were going to see our son born; he was going to be born alive, but he was not going to live.

I grabbed the doctor in the hall to clarify a few things that were not sitting well inside of me. "What do you mean that he will be born alive but will not live? Are you sure? Is there nothing we can do? We have insurance. We have good jobs."

And then, more slowly, "How long does it take to die?"

See, I have never told anyone this, but I could sense surprise with hospital staff during this entire pregnancy: surprise that I was White and she was Black. I see people posting pictures on Facebook all the time of premature babies, calling them miracles and gifts. Why the f**k can't this be the same? Is this a color thing? My brain went there and if mine did, I am guessing others did as well.

In my head, I kept saying, What the f**k you mean, our baby boy is going to be born and he is going to die?

My girlfriend was a beautiful, strong woman, a church woman who prided herself on her family's closeness. As she was taken to the birthing room, family and close friends started to arrive one by one, all with looks of worry and concern. Her pastor showed up and so did her brother, whom I respect.

The room was dark, gloomily lit, and everyone took their strategic spots, like a team. I knew she needed that closeness and was so happy that all those people showed up. Respectfully, I sat in the corner. My legs were weak and my stomach was sick, but I put on a mask of strength. This wasn't the time to be a weak man, but weakness and strength battled in my mind like caged lions. The room was full of beautiful Blackness handling the situation like they were trained for this. It was just an example of real love.

The doctor came in and began to induce the birthing process. Time seemed to tick slow. We all wanted our loved one to be okay but knew that all our lives were about to change forever. Life would never look the same. I could feel the learning experience on its way and our bodies naturally preparing for it.

The pastor prayed with her and rubbed her as our baby boy arrived. She had prepared for this time and asked to have the baby removed from the room when he was born. That was smart for her mental wellness.

When the baby was born, he was handed to the pastor. I followed him and the elders down the hall to a quiet room. It was an old, dimly lit room that had seen better days and looked like a classroom that students had messed up. As the pastor walked, he lightly sang what I think were old church spirituals, softly into my son's ears. I didn't mind that he was carrying my son and singing because with death around the corner, I wanted him to feel that Godly love.

We all sat in the room. Her auntie held him for several minutes, praying, singing, and smiling to him.

"He looks like you," someone said.

"He is beautiful," said another.

Then the auntie said, "It is time for us all to leave him alone with his father."

She handed me my son and I began to whimper tears I'd never felt before. It was a different emotion, a mixture of defeat, obligation, pride, and deep love.

About every five or ten minutes, a nurse would come in the room and check my son's vitals. As she would leave, I would ask the same questions, "Isn't there something you can do? How long does this take?"

"It can take anywhere from five to 25 minutes." The nurse kept saying, "I am sorry, but his lungs are just not strong enough."

This was no time for chit-chat. These were the moments to spend with my son while I had him.

I undid his blue blanket a little bit and slowly pulled him near my face and whispered in his ear. I sang him songs and told him about his mother and me and what type of people we are, how much we love him, and how honored we are to be his parents.

Time continued to tick. I continued to study my son, like only a father can. His little muscles were formed. Occasionally he would stretch them slowly. As we approached about an hour, his breaths started to appear labored, and I raced to tell him everything he needed to know for his journey. I made him a promise that I will always keep.

"God is with you, little man. Daddy and Mommy love you. Baby boy, I promise you, for the rest of my life, Daddy will carry you so deep in his heart with everything that he does. I promise you that I will do heavenly work in honor of your name. I will give myself to other little boys who look like you and invest in their lives. I hope you hear me, son, because Daddy keeps his promises. I will never forget you and I got your back through the rest of this journey until you go to meet our Father."

I kissed him one last time and held him high in the air as his breaths came harder and harder. Held in the air high. On top of the world. *Our Father, who art in heaven... Please, Grandmaw, have the Lord take him now...as we forgive those who trespass against us.*

J A, my son, took a deep breath and was gone.

Time. It doesn't matter if someone is in your life for a minute, a day, a month, or 100 years. That life can impact you forever. My son taught me on October 11, 2013, more than most have taught me in a lifetime. He taught me the definition of life, the precious closeness of real love, the warmth of human touch, and the gift of time.

He is buried in a beautiful park near other angels like him. I spend some of my time there when I need to talk and get real with myself. I stop through on my way to work, after work, and even in the snow. I have taken him footballs and candy, and even his allowance on occasion.

A few months after his death, I had a vision. Not a thought, a vision, like our Native people talk about. I have had sacred visions before and have even talked to indigenous brothers about them to get a better understanding and respectfully appreciate the importance behind the vision. I learned of true stories of wildlife walking up to the hunter to be petted and loved. I have seen the messengers on several occasions: most were wild animals. The vision makes you feel the presence of others who are no longer here. It's not scary; it's real and warm and it speaks for itself.

The vision I had following his passing came to me after talking to an old homeless woman who had cancer. She was sitting outside a store, in a wheelchair, wrapped in a blanket. I had nothing to get at the store that day but as I drove past, through the slushy snow, something told me to pull into the parking lot. I know a lot of people and I had never seen her before. I never saw her again after our meeting. I could tell she was chilled as I approached her, so I decided to go back to the car to get her a hat and gloves that were in the back.

I sat with her as she asked passers-by for change. I grabbed her up in my arms to help her get a little warmer. We sat for a long time and even laughed together for a spell. I could see the beauty behind her toothless smile.

She laughed deeply when she said, "Big football player-looking man like you probably going in there to buy up the whole store."

"No, mam. A higher power told me to stop to check on you."

Gentle smile. "I know He did."

I gave her what money I had in my pocket, kissed her forehead goodbye, and walked towards the car.

A voice in my head said, "Good job, Daddy."

I responded, "Thanks, J A," and just kept it moving.

OH, THAT VASECTOMY

I had talked with my friends about having a vasectomy. They said, "Just do it. It is real easy. You go in, get snipped, leave, ice the area for a day or two, and it is all over with.

So off I went to a clinic. The clipping wasn't done in a surgical environment like what I was used to from my heart surgeries. It seemed like a closet area. It was the strangest thing ever. Just one step above a gas station bathroom or a back alley. Well, maybe not, but that is what it felt like to me.

The vasectomy did not go like my friends had said. I was sitting at home after the procedure and my testicles started to swell. To the size of grapefruits. This was not good at all. Infection.

I went to the ER two or three times, and they kept saying, "Go home and ice the area." On my final time in the ER, the doctor had been a Marine. When he came into the room, I immediately asked for oxycodone. I think he thought I was joking, but then started getting all military stern with me saying, "You don't need this."

The male nurse in the room said, "Uh, sir, you might want to look at what we have going on here before you continue."

The military doctor pulled my pants down a little bit, saw the swelling, and got on the phone instantaneously. I received all kinds of medicine. The tough Marine said, "You poor guy. I'm so sorry!"

Then I had to go in for surgery to drain the fluid and blood and all that stuff. I told them I did not want visitors. I did not want flowers. I did not want anybody to know other than my parents. None of that.

My testicles were so big that when they were taking me from the hospital bed to put me on the surgery table, I told them to leave me alone and I would move myself because the pain was so bad. As we were going across to the other table, they grabbed and pulled me. My balls fell between the two tables and got caught up. Actually caught. That roar you heard did not come from the lion in the Vilas Zoo. Those were some big balls.

I was in the hospital longer for my testicles than I was following my heart surgery. Then I was off work for about three months with my feet up in the air. It was truly worse than heart surgery! It was the most painful experience. I gained a huge, huge respect for what women go

129

through with childbirth because, to have what I had going on down there and then having to push out a seven-pound object, well...

Joshlynn had gotten a kitten at this time, and it loved to pounce. On me. When I was home alone, sitting in my recliner with my ice pack, this cat would come out of nowhere, for some reason, and pounce right on that area. That cat lives with Joshlynn's mother now. No more pouncing on me.

The hospital called me after my recovery asking for a semen sample to make sure the vasectomy had worked. I told them that, after this experience, if I have another child, it's supposed to be here. I'm not giving a sample of nothing!

FOOTBALL—MATEO AND THE SOUTHSIDE RAIDERS YOUTH FOOTBALL AND CHEERLEADER PROGRAM

I promise you that I will do heavenly work in honor of your name. I will give myself to other little boys who look like you and invest in their lives. I hope you hear me, son, because Daddy keeps his promises.

I began coaching football with the Southside Raiders Youth Football and Cheerleader Program in Madison.

What can dislodge prostitution, drug sales, and violence in a marginalized neighborhood park? Pride. Respect. The Southside Raiders' football crowds at Madison's Penn Park are as energetically supportive as any UW Badgers or NFL fans. But it is also true that this sort of community support needs to be continuous, or the pride, respect, and safety can vanish. Negative things could still happen if support declines.

It is interesting to watch fans from an opposing team come to the Penn Park games. They arrive a little late and they leave real quick after. The thing they don't realize is that the park they are afraid of is probably the safest place they can be because nobody is going to allow anything to happen in Penn Park during practices or games. If anyone tried to pull a trigger or something like that, they would have a rain of s**t coming down on them.

Youth dreams are alive with the Southside Raiders. You are going to see aggressive playing. Sometimes the opposing team gets their collective ass smacked in ways they are not used to. The Raiders hit hard, but they hit fair.

At the same time, the kids must pull back at times. For example, the linebackers may have to step farther away from the line to avoid getting penalty calls for being too close. Racism rears up even in children's sports. They can be targets. Unfortunately. The kids need to be mindful.

Many of these southside kids are coming from single-parent homes or adverse environments. Penn Park is the happy place where they get guidance and have their feel-good time: atta-boys and atta-girls. They learn how to win.

And lose.

For some of these kids, the Raiders are all they have. When the team loses a game, they can lose hope.

A lot is being learned on that field aside from football, things like discipline, teamwork, and treatment of others. "This is the best game in town," I tell the kids. They are at crossroads in 4th, 5th, 6th, and 7th grades. By 8th grade, they are headed to high school and, in the best-case scenario, they either stick it out and become members of the fraternity of football players or possibly focus on being a student.

But in an impoverished community, these 8th graders are coming of age. Older guys may see them as a lookout or someone to run the bag up and down the street. It is a testing ground and a perfect time for young men to be grabbed and eaten by a gang. They are so vulnerable.

P was in 8th grade. He had matured early. His mom cared so deeply about him succeeding in school and would even come to football practice and take him home to study if he had gotten a bad grade. Little Black kids can be so cute with their tiny hands and soft hair. Adorable. But when they get to the size P was with man muscles, their hands and bodies are no longer cute. Fear-worthy. I went to Penn Park one day and saw a hoop game going on. P was in the mix. He had skipped school and was playing with adult men he should not have been around. An intelligent kid. A kid who matured early. And a kid who is now on his way to prison.

* * *

Mateo was an 8th grader when we met at the Southside Raiders Youth Football and Cheerleader Program. He was showing up daily.

Some volunteers, after learning about my kicking and punting background, said, "Joshua sounds like a good guy for Mateo." The talk continued about this southside Mexican kid whose parents were real busy with their grocery and food truck businesses. His family kept him on the grind, but he was still at a vulnerable stage and could have gotten sucked into a gang.

The volunteers felt bad for him, pitied him because he had been born with only one hand.

A volunteer asked me, "Can you come to practice after work?"

"Sure."

I came the following week, dressed in a sports coat—my work clothes. The coach introduced me to this big, tall Mexican kid, explaining, "Coach will give you a few tips on kicking and punting; how to get the ball on the line."

Was Mateo serious? Eager? I wanted to get into his head a little bit. Who was he? How much did he want to do this? What were his goals?

As we talked, I could tell he wanted to be a part of that crowd and be an asset to his team. I could also see that the rest of the team loved him. He knew how to talk s**t and be in the mix. His heart and mind were in this. I could relate.

He was very open about his one hand; he never hid it or anything. I told him that his hand did not bother me at all because my cousin was born with the same birth defect, and she played basketball and piano. I told him why I had become a punter. Mateo and I came together from day one and I promised him that I would be at every practice from then on to make sure he had the skills he needed to reach his goals.

Second practice. He said, "I'm sorry, my f**kin' shirt smells like enchiladas; I grabbed the wrong T-shirt." It was his brother's shirt from the night before when the family was cooking for the businesses.

As we practiced, I realized there were a few things he couldn't do, but when he looked down at his shoes, I said, "Mateo, we are going to have to get some kicking shoes."

He replied, "No, Coach. I just need you to tie my shoe."

Tying his shoes was something I got used to doing; sometimes too tight and I'd have to do it over again. As our relationship deepened, we were speaking a shared language and it was almost like I became a part of his body. Our trust was total, fluent.

I took Mateo to a kicking camp in Minneapolis. He jumped in the punting line to do live snaps. We had practiced field-goal kicking and played some catch but had not worked on live snaps.

Well, he bangs one.

On the drive home, he told me, "I like kicking and all, but I really want to be a punter and go to college." That was the day I realized: Now I'm riding with "me." It was one of the most beautiful feelings I've ever had, seeing that I was like the guys who had sat next to 8th-grade-me, guiding me, and encouraging me.

We talked about my heart problems and how the only difference between us was that my disability was invisible. But it was the same thing and I'd always felt that I was lesser than. It was a feeling of, *You can't do whatever because of this*. I said, "Well, my disability made me hungry."

He replied, "Coach, I'm hungry. I'm going to listen to everything you say."

I was able to be at every practice and game with Mateo. He solidified his spot on his high school team and ended up winning some games because of his skill. He even brought some southside swagger to the game. Every time he went out for the team kickoff with his hand in the air, he yelled out, "Everybody, let's eat." I played a father role for him more than once; I had his back. I don't f**k around when it comes to this young man. I am so proud of him.

His family had to work long hours in their businesses. They speak Spanish. I began showing up at the grocery store, meeting him there, and having lunch. I wanted to show his family that I was a genuine human being helping their son succeed. I started putting on weight and was teasingly told I was eating too many tortillas, Mexican Cokes, and tacos. His family loves him so much and have helped him be assured in who he is. (He always has the nicest shoes and sometimes even wears Ugg boots…now that is confidence!) The family love and respect are mutual, and they even began to include me. I knew nothing would ever happen to me in that store. Mateo told me he wanted to be successful in sports or business, so his mom wouldn't have to work so hard.

* * *

During this time, I led a high school group for boys of color to help them deal with the racial inequities and the daily struggles of being a young man. I invited Mateo to join, and he did. When a young man respects his coach, he will never call him by his first name. Never. It is always, "Coach." I felt I had that coach-grip on Mateo, who could even tell me, "I love you, Coach."

Then Tony Robinson was killed by a Madison police officer. This young Black man was acting erratically, the police report said. He died from seven bullets fired from the zero to five-foot range.

The boys in my group totally focused on Tony's killing. These kids were feeling that pain daily from the tops of their heads to the bottoms of their toes. The pain was vivid in their eyes. Mateo wondered, "Could this happen to me because I'm Brown? Could they take my life?"

What could I say?

Mateo drove the family BMW with tinted windows. He drove a nicer car than I did, and it came from hard-working people. Could he be racially profiled because of what his parents had provided for him? Could he get accused of being a drug dealer or something and get smoked by a cop? Could I lose him? That s**t really twisted me, even with my criminal justice background.

Why had the Madison police officer followed Tony Robinson into the house? Why not call for back-up and try to talk Tony out? I wasn't there but I have seen some bad s**t happen. I had a little bit of empathy for the officer and do not believe he was out to kill a Black kid on that day, or at least I would hope not. At some point though, the officer must have completely lost every bit of training. Maybe he was having his own trauma when he pulled the gun. I expect he is hurting even now, although I don't know.

But it was terrible. Regardless of what the situation was, the community lost someone. A young man was killed that day. Tony Robinson died.

My Gang Response Intervention Team partner and I worked with our boys, hoping they could protest safely. We walked with them downtown as the helicopters surged overhead. I'm pretty sure the police had sniper teams in place. We wanted the boys to feel love and support during this tough time.

We had talked with them about survival rules on how to act with a police officer: be respectful, don't argue, keep your hands in plain sight and out of your pockets, avoid all physical contact, make no sudden movements, do not resist arrest, do not run, stay calm, in control, and ask for a parent to be involved (especially during an interrogation).

Around 1,500 protesters, mostly high school students, went to the Wisconsin State Capitol yelling, "Hands up, don't shoot." The Capitol rotunda erupted with the call, "What's his name? Say his name?" That man had a name. It doesn't matter what drugs he might have been on. The protesters were seeing a young Black man who looked like them. It could have gotten really ugly. There was so much hurt.

I saw one kid who had formerly been in our program. His eyes were red and swollen. I asked him, "Are you okay?" He leaned in and grabbed a hold of me and said, "I need a hug. Tony was my friend." I could actually feel his body quivering.

In the Capitol building, my legs got weak. I felt like crying out, but my cry was, "It was about time; we have had enough." I felt really bad about Tony's death but at the same time I was so glad to see officers brought to the table. It really hit me that we live in two different worlds.

As the protests evolved, more organizations started taking note of what was happening in Madison. I think this was the first time Black Lives Matter showed its face in the city. Mike Brown got killed about this same time in Ferguson, Missouri. I sensed people felt they needed to prepare because racism was rising up throughout the country.

One of the Madison neighborhood officers, who volunteered with youth, came up to talk to me at the Penn Park basketball court. The kids turned their backs. He got the spin-off from everyone.

I asked Mateo to shake the officer's hand. He said, "I ain't f**king s**t shaking his hand." I explained that this cop had nothing to do with Tony's death. Mateo did not want to do it, but finally offered a weak handshake. He said, "I only do this out of respect for you, Coach, but I ain't feeling these police right now. To me they are a bunch of bulls**t."

I hadn't ever heard him talk like that.

* * *

I got an email from the mother of one of the mixed-race boys I had coached. She was remarried to a White cop. She and her husband thought I was siding...siding against the police. She yanked her boy away from me. (About six months later, I got an apology when they recognized my background and my authenticity.)

But that really hurt. I found myself second-guessing policing. Is this actually how the world thinks? Do we take sides like this? Do we just go tit-for-tat? I'm White. I have been formally educated on policing in America. I graduated from a police academy and was president of the class. I have worked as a parole officer, a prison guard, and in a gang prevention unit.

My relationship with these boys has nothing to do with all of this. I also know that what comes out of my mouth is the truth. I'm with the boys to the end. I ride the line. We ride the line together.

Mateo was admitted to the University of Wisconsin PEOPLE Program, an opportunity for lower-income, often first-generation youth to go to college, usually at the flagship University of Wisconsin–Madison. The five-year program prepares these committed youth to be viable candidates, eligible for a four-year tuition scholarship. Mateo wanted to punt for the UW Badgers but ended up at the Division III UW–Platteville campus for one year. He then transferred to UW–Madison, where he is now majoring in business so he can help his family.

I think he will still have an opportunity to punt the ball for the UW Badgers. He has the swagger and confidence and skill of a Division I athlete who is all business.

His story is not over.

IMAGINE A WORLD WHERE ALL BLACK PEOPLE
LIVE WITHOUT FEAR OR LIMITATION

In my gang intervention work these days, I know I help boys navigate racial, historical, and economic obstacles.

It saddens me that there must be such a job. Madison stats are so horrible. It blows my mind that we need to have all these trainings on implicit bias and racial healing because obviously we are lacking. People have gotten hired for these professional jobs and don't know how to treat another human being yet. Good that the city is being progressive, but they should have done this a long time ago. It is just sad.

Madison has racial problems. It is a tale of two cities: haves and have-nots. Some of the do-gooders toss money at problems just so they can say they did their piece, without even checking to see if the organizations they are supporting are doing anything valuable. Money is only the top layer, and it will never do enough. Relationships are what is going to make a difference. We all need to come together and carry-on conversations.

I live on the South Side and have heard people, who don't know where I live, say they would never stop at McDonalds or buy gas near my home. This is part of our failure. We cannot expect things to change if we don't know each other as humans. Too many of us aren't exposed to differences. Are we afraid? Do we feel we don't have time for deeper, honest relationships? Like Mateo and me. If he is ever killed, I am going to hurt like I've lost my son.

There is also another layer of challenge in making change. It isn't all wealthy Whites. When there is a problem, like the killing of Tony Robinson, you will get a real clear view of what I call "poverty pimps." They take a major issue and utilize it to raise money. Just watch how quickly they can race to get their face out there: a crab in the bucket mentality. They could make this an Olympic event!

Booker T. Washington explained this in his 1901 book, *Up From Slavery:* "There is a certain class of race-problem solvers who don't want the patient to get well because, as long as the disease holds out, they have not only an easy means of making a living but also an easy medium through which to make themselves prominent before the public."

I've never feared crossing the lines of difference, of all kinds. I told my parents when I was considering being a law enforcement officer that if I was ever killed by a Black man, "Don't hate; it's just what happened. Don't hate all Blacks because of the actions of one man." It blows my mind that such a simple thing as skin pigment has ruined our world. It's like the difference between Coke and Pepsi. How can so many of us be so obtuse? So stupid?

* * *

Some of my kids tease me. I take it as a sign of respect, like a kind of shared scenario of their lives that forever connects us. A PTSD we have been through together. I hope I'm right about that!

One day, I was driving down the Beltline and exited at Stoughton Road. A Cadillac was following me. I stopped at a light and one of the black-tinted windows was lowered real slow, like just enough room for a gun to come out. My heart started pounding. Turned out it was my boys, and they knew what they were doing; scared the hell out of me. Teasing.

Another time, I was walking across Memorial High School's parking lot after a football game. It was dark. A car pulled up alongside of me. Same scenario. Black-tinted windows. A voice said, "Empty your pockets, n****."

I was like, "Oh s**t, I'm getting robbed."

It was my boys again.

I will also get emails or calls from my boys like, "Hey, man, you gotta come over to my granny's and see my son." That kind of invitation gives me a good feeling.

And one other story. I took a very challenged boy to a movie once. He had gotten into leaded paint in their Chicago apartment and had brain damage. It was just the two of us in the theater. During the movie, a Black woman was being beaten. He screamed out, "No!"

I knew his mom had died. At that moment, he leaned over and put his head on my shoulder. He looked up at me, saying, "This is what it would be like if I had a dad." There was no way in hell I was going to tell him he needed to take his head off my shoulder.

A lot of people think it's weird that I tell these boys I love them. But, for me, it is not weird because I know for a fact that some of them have never heard it the way it is meant to be. When one of their friends gets hurt or dies out in the streets, I ask them, "Please don't do anything because if that happens to you, I don't know how I'll react. I don't know what that will do to my life because I do love you. If something happens to you, it is going to hurt me like you are my own kid."

Terrible things keep happening to these kids, whether it is a crime and their picture ends up in the paper or their friend gets shot or whatever; it all weighs heavy. These kids are my babies. These kids are the people I spend my time with, trying to guide them into a different direction.

JOSHUA'S KIDS—
MATERIALISM/GREED/JEALOUSY/MUSIC

I am realizing that writing a book may be like writing any genre of music. You must feel it run through your body; telling the stories of what you are deeply passionate about.

I care so much for these kids who are caught up in forces they do not see or comprehend. They are my job, my life.

My mother and I went out to get lunch. We dropped the top of the Jeep and let the sun beat on our faces. We turned on good music and pulled away.

About 200 yards from my house, I saw a woman pushing a cart. Under my breath, I said, "There is a dead body."

My mother heard me, "What did you say? Turn around."

"That's not a good idea."

"No, turn around."

As we came back around the corner, the body wrapped in a red velvet bag was being loaded into a rusty van. It took very little effort to lift the tiny person. There is a police station less than 100 feet away and a squad car was parked up the street. Another squad was driving slowly as the officer appeared to be trying to talk with a young man I'd never seen before.

My mother's eyes filled with tears and she began to pray. She whimpered to me that she had seen old people die before but this was different. It could have been an old lady, a covid death, a suicide, or anything really, but the chances were high it was an overdose of heroin or fentanyl given that we were in town and the small body size.

My hood intelligence told me the young man walking past, watching, was probably the dealer who sold the bag. He wanted to see what was up. The building behind them is a known "trap house" (one way in, one way out) where a lot of my clients have relapsed in the past.

The grisly cycle persists.

* * *

I am feeling the beat of this loss, this death, in my heart today. I want to say something around how materialism, jealousy, greed, and the message of music impacts our kids. I want to bring some humanity to this person's death. The streets have taught me so much about our human plight and where too many are heading. I feel a higher power wants me to view these mind-damaging encounters so I can teach others, hoping they can be spared.

My opinion? There is nothing in these streets that will ever develop a wealthy, happy human being. These streets are where fear meets fear, trauma walks laps, tears rain down, and smiles are too often fake.

MATERIALISM (a tendency to consider material possessions and bodily comfort as more important than spiritual ideals).

Daily, whether it be through personal contact with the kids I work with, or on their Facebook site postings, I hear and see things I feel are damaging.

- "I am the plug."
- "Let's get this bag."
- "I am a Trap Star."
- "Ghetto Superstar."
- "I'm going to catch you in traffic."
- "I make more money in a week than the teacher makes in six months."

These phrases come from young men and women who are often wearing top to bottom designer clothing and holding handfuls of money, but usually standing in some dusty apartment building.

I asked one young man what he wanted for his birthday. His answer? "Gucci flip-flops." I didn't think that was a big ask until I looked online and saw they ranged from $400 up.

I get it. Because of my heart condition, my mother spoiled me. She made sure I had designer clothing: Jordans and the best cologne. Why? She did not have to do this. Did she think these things would make me popular? Did she feel sorry that I had a heart problem and wanted me to shine every day?

As a man who has knocked on Heaven's door, I will tell you that at the end, it doesn't matter if you go out with Gucci flip-flops or barefooted. One thing is certain, at that point you're not worried about material things.

Why do we want like this? Things. We are all guilty, but I think it's especially damaging to youth and people who are struggling financially. Just like my mother was trying to make me feel better, so many moms attempt to do the same in the hood.

My grandpaw was 97 years old when he died this year. He had a cream-colored Cadillac in his garage. A 1991 with under 40,000 miles on it. Cream leather seats and a blue rag top. It still smells new.

He had always liked nice cars and looks so proud sitting in them, a big smile with a gold-tooth shine.

He had caught a fever at a young age and became deaf. His dad died early, and Grandpaw ran the farm by himself from age 13 on. He raised his siblings and made sure their needs were met, even though the family was economically poor. He became the man.

Grandpaw was looked down on for being deaf. He was seen as dumb even though he was very smart.

That Cadillac and all the nice cars before it? They were about him letting the jungle know, "I am here. I matter."

Objects equating to earthly value. I do get it. And yet I see the set up.

Many of us are guilty because we too often place things before people. We are quick to base success on financial wealth. The need to have more and more is damaging us on so many levels and we are too blind to see it.

GREED *(an intense and selfish desire for something—notably wealth, power, or food).*

So, you think you the plug? The head boss man, huh?

Let's keep it real. You not.

Do you know how many drug dealers I have met in my life? Can't count them all. Every ethnicity and all with similar stories. They always have regret after they get a wake-up call (if they're lucky enough to wake up after the call, that is).

Some make as much money as NFL players. Some make enough for a new pair of Jordans. But none were the plug.

Just like any business, the disenfranchised take the punishment while filling someone else's pockets. Often, that someone else doesn't live in this country, doesn't look like you, and you will never meet him or her. If you don't believe me, go on the DEA's Most Wanted List, and see who they are looking for. I bet it's not you or anyone you know. But it is you who gets killed, you who fills the prisons, and you they are banking on to get the chore done.

My partner and I were once working with a young man we really liked, a very polite kid with big dreams. He wanted to own a barbershop. He also loved the latest fads.

He was a homeless kid who was a couch-surfer and always looking for his next meal. He was next to zero for family support but was well liked among his peers.

And the streets were showing him love early on.

As he matured, it was not clear where reality would take him. My partner and I were in his ear, competing with the streets. He was in one of our boys' groups and attended consistently, each week.

On the final day of the group meeting, he wanted to tell us something. We could tell it weighed heavily on him. To our surprise, he told us that he never attended his high school classes; he only came to our group. He loved our conversations because they made him think deeply. He enjoyed the relationships, the meals, and that exciting opportunities he had to volunteer with children.

My partner and I realized we had unintentionally missed critical things. It dawned on us too late. We said, "F**k," at the same time. We assumed he was doing better than normal. He smiled more. We hadn't noticed his gradually increasing wardrobe. We hadn't noticed he was missing school because he was there when we were. His name wasn't coming up among school staff or law enforcement. We hadn't even checked his Facebook page because we were certain he was okay and staying out the way of the streets.

When I got home, I looked up his page. There it was. He was with the best team and getting the bag. There were photos of him with stacks of money, standing by nice cars, and posting that he was the man. Greed was winning.

I phoned him. He answered and said he'd call me back. He never did. The next day, I checked his last known address. The lady who answered said she thought he took a trip to Illinois and would be back before the weekend.

A few weeks later, I saw him at a stoplight. He was clearly in those streets. Deep. I would say he was on his tiptoes and the water level was just under his nose. But he was driving a new Audi and wearing Gucci flip-flops. Gucci bag. Gucci suit. Man, did he look good, feel good, and smell good. You want it. He got it.

* * *

Who dropped the ball? Who's to blame? Why does this happen? Was it just myself and my partner's failure?

Again, I am going to keep it real and only voice my opinion in hopes it sparks conversation to better the situation that is a constant with many youth and young adults. Just throwing out thought-provoking ideas and I don't mean to offend anyone.

But what the f**k did we think would happen? This kid was raised by the streets and was taking notes. He was taking notes from my partner and me also, but we were only with him an hour a week. He wasn't involved in sports, band, choir, or the school newspaper where he had a story to tell.

He was out there trying to survive, looking for his next meal, and wondering where he was going to stay. The way I look at it, he got tired of not being heard. He got tired of wearing the same pants every day. He got tired of depending on rides and asking people to buy him a sandwich when he was hungry. You can only ignore the gorilla in the jungle for so long before he lets you know he is there, and that he is running s**t.

He was greedy to survive and did so in the ways he understood.

This helping business so many of us are involved in is based on outcomes, not dollars. It is based on human life. Having been in the streets for a minute now, I can pretty much accurately guess the outcome of this boy's situation. We will likely see him laid out in the street with handcuffs on or a chalk line around his body.

I am tired of seeing *Rest in Peace, Ball in Paradise, Fly High my Boy* on people's Facebook pages. I am tired of seeing balloon releases at the homicide site and tired of seeing Go Fund Me accounts being set up for another senseless funeral. Teddy bears by telephone poles. Liquor bottles curbside with burnt out candles.

I am tired of that. So tired.

JEALOUSY (a feeling or state of resentment, bitterness, or hostility toward someone because they have something you don't).
You know what gets drug dealers arrested or killed?

Their "brothers."

Do you know why?

Jealousy and envy (that's my opinion).

Let's face it, it doesn't matter if you are in the trailer park, ghetto, barrio, or living in a homeless encampment. Someone wants what they don't or can't have, creating jealousy and envy. Both are forms of mental illness. You know what people who are ill with jealousy and envy hate the most? They hate when you shove at them what you have and they don't, often through Facebook or social media.

Yes, Facebook is a caring place where you can see your loved ones, read about their latest vacation, the new baby, and even that great dinner they had last evening. Wonderful connection tools to keep us updated on everyone's lives.

It is also a place to show off your money, cars, women/men, and newest gun with a drum attached so instead of 12 rounds, now you can set it off with 100.

Everybody and their dog is on some form of social media. Your "opposition" (opp) is on there too and there is a high chance your opp is either a friend you didn't know was an opp or a friend who hangs with your opps and they are jealous and envious of what you got. Especially your drugs and money.

I would be interested in knowing how many people have died from gun violence in the last 25 years with a pair of Jordans on their feet.

MUSIC (vocal or instrumental sounds, separate or combined in such a way as to produce beauty of form, harmony, and expression of sentiment).

The voice of the people. Music messages set the tone for our day, our next adventure, our stories of the good times, and bad. It reminds us. Is it a natural drug that sets the mood from our central nervous system? Is a piece of our brain specially designed for music, connected to our emotions?

Have you thought about music and how it impacts us? I have utilized a different music genre for each portion of this book as I write and ponder my words. For example, if I am writing about the people and stories from back home, Lancaster, I listen to Mississippi blues or country music that reminds me of those moments in my life, from football pump up music that makes me high to sad songs that make me cry. Music is a part of the stories.

Most generations have had to deal with the struggle of older adults not understanding the new music, their music, their tales. If we are truly invested in our youth and love them, we must listen to their language, their music, even if we don't like it.

There are messages in some of the youth music telling us about injuries, tiredness, or readiness for whatever comes their way. Drill music isn't a fad; it's an honest expression of what they are feeling, and it offers a platform to express what they are seeing. Most adults today will never be introduced to this form of music or understand the messages. Not a part of their reality.

But the music of youth is a part of me and my job. It's a must that I be fluent in their language, their truth.

Just like a country song tells us about the fields needing rain and R&B asks what's going on, drill rap is an expression of what is being seen, felt, and heard. It's a tribal pulse that delivers war chants of pain and struggle. It tells us about the identity of certain people living in the struggle and where they feel they stand as citizens. It informs on who is the rat, tells us who is the next victim (often using their name), who they hate, and why they hate them. It's the pulse of the streets.

Knowing it could save a life.

If you listen, you will quickly realize that the hood has its own appointed mayor, police force, banking system, and laws. This is what happens when you disenfranchise people, push them aside, treat them like foreigners, and when they don't get their piece of the pie. They build their own, yah dig?

Why?

I am emotional right now writing this and I will not tell you what I am listening to because I don't want to have a tribe after me. Real talk. However, I do have to tell you that I can appreciate the message. I hear your cries. I see your weapons and know that each of you are truly hurt by the position society has placed you in.

I do my best to help others listen so they can understand, even if they don't want to. We can hear the cries for help by listening to these tribal songs. With social media, the cries go out fast. But know one thing for certain. I am tired of the pain.

I recently listened to a song that a kid had put some names in. I called him right away because he put himself at risk. He may still be …

* * *

And what can self-centeredness lead to as we focus on our own materialism, greed, jealousy, and music? Some people will say the following:

- This kid in the streets isn't my problem.
- He or she should have had a job.
- Is it my fault he didn't graduate?
- Where were his parents?

"It has nothing to do with me and my life. How does this affect me?" you may ask.

I am glad it doesn't affect you now. But it will. It will when your daughter who is a paramedic calls you at 1am sounding intoxicated. She needs to talk, and you find out that two hours ago, she held a child in her arms watching him die. She wants to tell you everything she experienced, like the hole on the side of his head and how you could see the bullet protrude right above his eye, but she can't go deep because it doesn't affect you.

Or when you see your patriotic son who just graduated from the police academy on the news. You told all your friends. You were so proud that you bought him a police medallion for his desk. You got a magnet with the words, "I support law enforcement" for the trunk of your car. And there he was on the news, standing by the yellow crime scene tape and you comment to your husband, "He looks so serious." You both laugh at that look — that WTF look he had. That was his face after seeing a carload of boys crash on the highway while running from rival gang members. What they didn't show on the news was the carnage he saw firsthand. Yes. He was serious, Mom. Does it affect you?

It's a Hood Shrine

Concrete slabs, blood-stained curbside
Tears, sobs, liquor bottles
It's a Hood shrine

A newly found sacred place, in the ghetto
Another Black boy, dead
Didn't you get the memo?

Concrete slabs, blood-stained curbside
Tears, sobs, liquor bottles
It's a Hood shrine

He was only twelve I heard them say
Wrong place, wrong time
As more bullets sprayed

Taped pictures of basketball games on the nearest pole
Tied balloons, tattoo tears
It took its toll

Concrete slabs, blood-stained curbside
Tears, sobs, liquor bottles
It's a Hood shrine
A place for his next birthday celebration

Only he won't be there
Permanent vacation

His mom screaming on the outside, and the inside
She screamed his life was set to start
Not end

Concrete slabs, blood-stained curbside
Tears, sobs, liquor bottles
Hood shrine
                        —Joshua Clauer

MY GRANDPAW—WHAT IT MEANS TO BE A MAN

I have always had the utmost admiration for my grandpaw, William Clauer. I share his name with my middle name and have always carried it with pride.

One of the purposes of this book was to write it before everyone has passed to the next life. It was important that I finished it so my grandpaw could read it and smile because life didn't offer him many smiles. A quiet and proud man with a touch of Napoleon syndrome that was always backed by strength.

As a boy I watched his every move and adopted it. Everything from how he put on his cap to how he spit tobacco, I mimicked. I heard many stories about my grandpaw's younger years and couldn't help but take my mind to old Western movies, young ranchers, saloon brawls, and tough cowboys. He was a heroic figure in my mind. Even though he couldn't hear much of anything his entire life, somehow he heard me often. I think he was a master lip reader, to be honest.

"You spit like this, see? That way it don't run down your cheek. But don't ever chew this stuff; it is not good for you!" (I did anyway.)

"Wear your hat like this, not backwards; it's meant to keep the sun out of your eyes!"

"Don't you ever let me hear that you fought with a gun, knife, or any other weapon. Those guys are not men, they cowards. Real men fight with their hands, their balance, and their wit." He was always proud to tell you how he tuned someone up for stepping out of bounds.

But not until the past few weeks did I realize how vulnerable he was throughout his entire life. Vulnerable with insecurities that were mentally crippling.

* * *

A few weeks ago, my dad found him bleeding out his mouth and obviously not feeling well. The ambulance came but Grandpaw did not want to go. During the following weeks, he had numerous tests, one being an MRI. When the doctor asked him if he was scared of the MRI, he replied, "S**t, I ain't never been scared of anything my entire life!"

His entire life he let the world know that he wasn't scared of s**t and if you crossed him, you would find out what kind of man he was. I heard the stories about some of the ass-whooping he laid out in his younger years and I even was on the other end of one once, but my grandmaw beat him off me. He was making sure that the old bull was teaching the baby bull who was boss.

I had never seen him weak before, ever. This time, he lay there so fragile, like a child. My grandmaw died a few years ago in the same hospital, after a fall. He had been miserable since she left us. Lonely and lost without her. She was his ears and loud so he could sometimes catch a little of the story. After she passed, I think he gave up on life because he had lost his best friend.

* * *

I went to see him the other day and he didn't always know me. He would go in and out of it. As I leaned up against his hospital bed in the dimly lit room, he smiled and asked, "Boy, what do you eat? You're big. Are you strong?"

"Yes, Grandpaw, I am strong," I said, as I swallowed back a few tears.

* * *

There is no way I was going to let him see me cry, not him! As I gazed into his eyes and inspected his body, I realized that at this point in life, he was handing over the keys to being a man to me. I felt it! I felt what it means to be a man and it's deep, deeper than any ocean.

His eyes filled with tears as he told me, for the millionth time, about his childhood. I listened like I never heard the story before. But I listened deeper than ever before because he was lying there wounded. I knew I may never hear the story again.

"I been deaf since I was eight. Can you imagine being deaf at the age of eight? Can't hear s**t, and everyone thinks you are dumb. It's like the world gives up on you. I was a smart man, and no one knew it; always thought I was dumb, but I wasn't. Can you imagine running a farm at the age of 12? S**t, kids today wouldn't understand that. I never got a chance to play."

Sometimes stories must be repeated over and over so that we get it. I've been hearing that story since I was a boy. I remember one Christmas, my parents bought me a bunch of gifts and Grandpaw took me in a room alone. He grabbed me sternly and told me to always respect my parents and to understand not everyone gets presents like that.

* * *

For 48 years, I have equated being a man with what society says a man is and have looked up to some of the toughest sons of bitches on the planet who I always thought couldn't be defeated no matter the circumstance and could handle anything thrown at them.

"Joshua, I don't know. I might be dying here. In four years, I will be 100. That seems like a long time from now, but it is crazy to think about how fast my life went. Where did the time go? So fast? I am either going home or to the cemetery."

"Either way, you are going home, Grandpaw," I said.

* * *

As I left the hospital, I felt a sadness that only true love knows and a sorrow that holds a wind that blows out candles. I was saying my last goodbyes to my grandpaw. Was giving my last handshake and final kiss to the forehead. Walking away with so many questions in my mind about life and why we have to love and die. Where do we go? Are their cornfields in heaven? Cowboys? Is my grandmaw waiting for him?

* * *

So, what does it mean to be a man?

A country plowboy, a farmer, a fighter, a mathematician, a lover, a dad, a grandpaw, a hard worker, and a highway man. Vulnerable, a victim, handicapped, tobacco chewing, no-tear-having Man!

It is only in his final hours that I am understanding what 48 years of love with my grandpaw have taught me about manhood:

- A man is wise enough to listen to his elders.
- A man never quits learning and realizes that, to get respect, you must give respect.
- A man never hides from his flaws or disabilities.
- A man doesn't need to be tough unless he must be tough to protect himself and his love.

- A man isn't defined by what kind of car he drives.

- A man isn't defined by how much money he has.

- A man loves his wife hard and protects her.

- A man realizes that his wife is his equal and allows for her to hold up the ship where the man is weak.

- A man realizes that love is real and never lets go of or damages what he loves.

- A man busts his ass for his family and truly doesn't come home until the work is done for the day.

- A man doesn't make friends by being angry and fighting the world.

- A man doesn't quit on himself and encourages others.

- A man leads youth by example and teaches them what he can, even the simplest of things.

- A man stands proud when a new member is born.

- A man knows that it's okay to release tears of joy and sadness and respects the release of power in each tear.

- A man leaves mother earth with dignity, knowing that he gave his all and,

- A man spits tobacco juice like this…

Thank you, Grandpaw. I love you!!!

FOOTBALL—
DEAR ARROW FOOTBALL COACHES,

I am writing you today to show my appreciation for you and everything you did for me as a young boy. Thank you for including me with your team. Everything that I learned from you and the coaching staff, I utilize today with the young men and women I work with. You and your staffs' teachings have honestly saved my life on several occasions. You gave me a winning spirit to keep going, knowing that I can be a champion at anything I put my mind to. I get it now and I think I am speaking for a lot of us.

When I met you guys, I must have been about 12 and it was a critical part of my life. My father was ill, I had this heart condition, and wasn't too good at school. My self-esteem was beaten up. I had a lot of stress that I was too young to explain, and I know you all knew that. Instead of pushing me aside and writing me off, you gave me an opportunity and showed, what I now know, was unconditional love. That unconditional love got me through my darkest hours as a kid. Y'all gave me the ability to dream.

The love shown toward me has directed me in life. I give that same love to others who may be feeling like I felt back then. I share the love that was given to me and pay it forward. Believe it or not, a few years ago, my partners and I had a client who committed an armed robbery in the eighth grade. We gave him the tools he needed to be a success, starting with the right shoes. We gave him support and love and, guess what? He graduated a year early and received a full-ride scholarship to a Division 1 school as a linebacker. We will see him on Sundays in the future.

You guys were so selfless with your time and, as a father, I do not know how you had the energy for all of us, as well as your own families. They deserve an award for all the time spent away from them. As boys, I don't think we understood how hard that was for all of you. Instead of being home with the ones you love, you chose to be with us.

I am writing this because it is the first time in my life I ever really paid attention to life's clock. Coaches, refs, and athletes don't control this ticker; it really stung when Coach M died, and I wish he was here to read this letter. He was a selfless man who gave everything — his best effort — and boy did he teach that! Don't you wish sometimes you could call a time-out on life? I sure do. Coach L was a hell of a man as well with so much kindness in his heart. A true gentle giant.

I was so happy that I was able to coach in the State Championship game with each of you in 2005. Such a great feeling it was to experience that with you. I needed that closeness during that part of my life. Had to get back to my roots for that moment in time. It got me ready for the days ahead. Lifted my spirits and got me back on track.

I am currently writing this book and a piece of it will tell our story because it should be told. Many can learn from it, I think. Not just athletes, coaches, and teachers but everyone, from police to bar owners. Our story sets an example for looking at life through a different lens by giving everyone a chance, like you did for me and so many others, regardless of any differences. The portion about us is a thank you from me. I am just blessed to be here to tell the story.

There is no-quit in me at this stage in my life and you all taught me that. You gave me a no-quit attitude even when there were signs of defeat. I still don't like pressure, but I have the tools to handle it. I look at the boys I work with now and see how vulnerable they are. Unfortunately, if sports don't want them, they turn to gangs for support. Some coaches don't understand where these kids are coming from and what they are going through. Many of the youth are looking for their next meal, some are homeless, most don't have fathers, and all are struggling.

One at a time.

When Covid hit, I was so scared to get it, with my heart condition, but now I have had both of my vaccinations. I hope you all have yours. Seeing all the death on the news both from the virus and from getting shot is so unsettling. Unfortunately, I am at risk for both of these at times, but I am built for it. Time doesn't stop for anyone and if my days are cut short, I want to make sure I show my love where love is due.

I love each of you, appreciate you, and want you to know that no matter where we are in our lives, you are often in my thoughts and prayers. Thank you for giving me your time in life. I will not let you down.

Sincerely,
Joshua W. Clauer (#88, the Punter)

POSTSCRIPT

FACEBOOK POST
OCTOBER 5, 2021 AT 4:50 AM

I wouldn't normally put my most personal, deepest, and trying times on social media! Life hands us many happy and exciting times with memories that will last a lifetime! Those memories stick there and bring back thoughts of much comfort!

Life also has a way of slowing us down, age us, and put us in some pretty adverse situations! I fell ill several weeks ago and I am once again being tested in this life! A lot of emotions surrounding this test because I have a lot more love I want to give and a lot more beautiful things I want to see! We must remember we don't dictate the test or it's results, we are only here to take it!!!

I appreciate all the thoughts and prayers from my family and closest of friends who I truly hold dear to my heart! Thank you! Your warmth and years of memories have brought me positive, uplifting thoughts during a time where it's hard to get to excited about much of anything!!

We are a Team! When one of us fights, we all start fighting too! Know whatever it is I got going on, I'm fighting because I have a lot to fight for!!!

I repeat Walter Payton's words: "Are you scared?"

"Hell, yeah I'm scared. Wouldn't you be scared?"

But it's not in my hands anymore. It's in God's hands.

Just prayers is all I need !!! We all can use them......love all of you reading this and may God keep you close!!!!

GLOSSARY

100 — to stay true; to be real; straight up.
https://www.urbandictionary.com/define.php?term=100

BAG — Large amount of money. https://www.urbandictionary.com/
define.php?term=A%20bag

COUCH SURFER — An adult who is homeless and finds various
couches to sleep on & homes to survive in until he/she is put out.
Or one who can NOT lease rental property for various reasons &
goes from couch to couch because their living situation is uncertain
day to day. https://www.urbandictionary.com/define.php?
term=Couch%20Surfer

DO-GOODER — An earnest, often naïve humanitarian or reformer
https://www.merriam-webster.com/dictionary/do-gooder

GANGBANGER — A member of a gang, who participates in gang
activity. This can be anything from graffiti to shooting up a rival
gang. https://www.urbandictionary.com/define.php?
term=gangbanger

G CARD — Informal accreditation of being a gangster. https://
www.urbandictionary.com/define.php?term=G-Card

OG — Original gangsta, someone who has been in a street gang for a
long time or is a very high rank member. https://
www.urbandictionary.com/define.php?term=OG

OPP — Opposition or the rival. https://www.urbandictionary.com/
define.php?term=opposition

PTSD — PTSD (Post-Traumatic Stress Disorder) is a mental health
problem that some people develop after experiencing or witnessing
a life-threatening event, like combat, a natural disaster, a car
accident, or sexual assault. It's normal to have upsetting memories,
feel on edge, or have trouble sleeping after this type of event. If
symptoms last more than a few months, it may be PTSD. The good
news is that there are effective treatments. https://www.ptsd.va.gov/

PLUG — A person who has everything you need. https://
www.urbandictionary.com/define.php?term=Plug

RICO — Passed in 1970, the Racketeer Influenced and Corrupt Organizations Act (RICO) is a federal law designed to combat organized crime in the United States. It allows prosecution and civil penalties for racketeering activity performed as part of an ongoing criminal enterprise. https://www.ussc.gov/guidelines/primers/rico

SET — Group of people, usually gang affiliated, for a particular neighborhood. https://www.urbandictionary.com/define.php?term=set

SPLIFF — A joint with tobacco and weed mixed together. https://www.urbandictionary.com/define.php?term=splif

STACK — $1000. https://www.urbandictionary.com/define.php?term=stacks

WTF — Generally stands for 'What the fuck'. Most people use a question mark afterwards to get the point through. https://www.urbandictionary.com/define.php?term=wtf

On Balance

Staff Spotlight – JOSHUA CLAUER, DC-NIP PROGRAM LEADER

For some people, a job is just a job... a way to make a living or to pass the time until retirement. But spend five minutes in the presence of Joshua Clauer and you can tell he feels very differently about his job. Joshua's commitment and enthusiasm for working with youth are immediately apparent.

Joshua began employment with the Dane County Neighborhood Intervention Program last May. In his Program Leader role, he works with youth at risk for gang involvement as well as those already involved. With co-worker George Brown, Joshua regularly conducts groups for for teen males which include, among other components, frank discussions about how gang behavior is a feeder to adult prison. Group sessions aim to build competency by providing participants with a variety of enrichment activities and experiences they might not otherwise have.

"I see a lot of kids being misled," Joshua says. The youth he works with need positive role models. He hopes to be that role model and to help them change in a positive direction. He wants kids to know they can dream, and that dreams can come true.

Joshua holds both a bachelors and masters degree in criminal justice. Most recently he was employed by Madison Area Urban Ministry assisting adults coming out of the prison system. Although he enjoyed that job, Joshua appreciates that his DC-NIP position allows him the opportunity to work with young men before they get deeper into the system.

Joshua has also worked for the WI Department of Corrections as a probation and parole agent with serious juvenile offender populations, an adult probation and parole agent in the gang and drug unit, and as a correctional sergeant at the Oregon Correctional Center. Those experiences, where he saw so much wasted talent, led him to change his focus to helping youth avoid that adult prison path.

When asked if he had any final comments, Joshua said, "I love this (work). I landed where I'm supposed to be." And, Joshua, we're certainly glad you did.

Dane County Human Services newsletter.

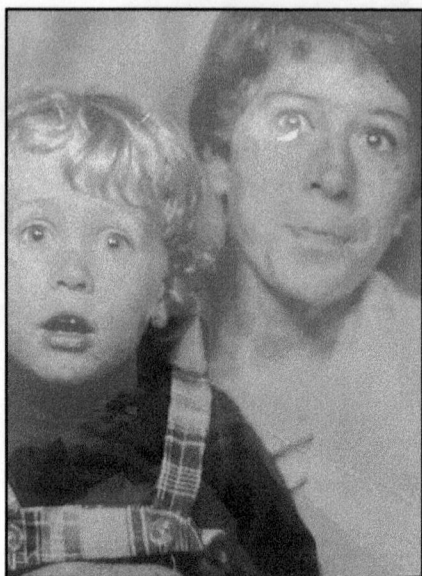

Joshua and his Maw.

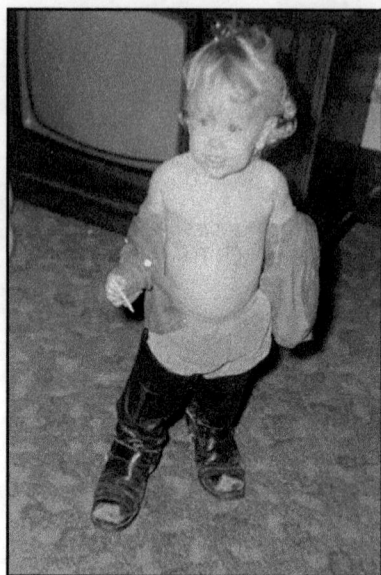

The kids at Triple R Ranch dressed up Joshua, added "Hi Mom" to his stomach and handed him a joint.

With Dad, climbing safely.

Joshua, the kid.

Joshua with Grandmaw Baus.

Traveling as a family, shortly before Dad went to the VA Hospital.

Baus Park in Lancaster, named after the family.

Earliest riding—Joshua is on the left.

A desert moon.

Posing at Sego Canyon, rock art and me (Dad and I smudged).

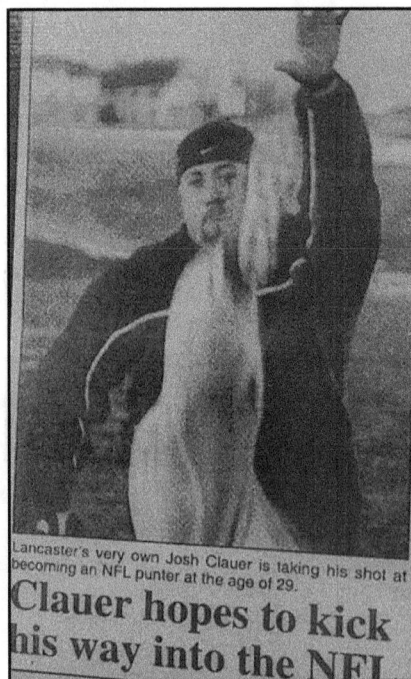

Lancaster's very own Josh Clauer is taking his shot at becoming an NFL punter at the age of 29.

Clauer hopes to kick his way into the NFL

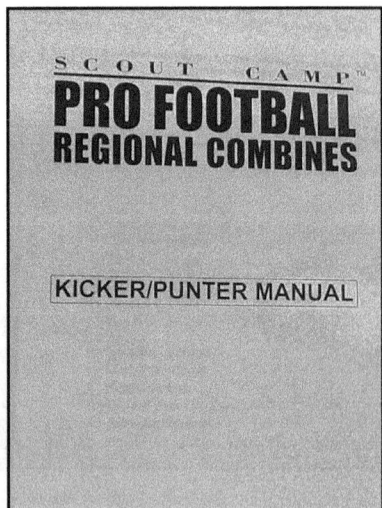

SCOUT CAMP
PRO FOOTBALL
REGIONAL COMBINES

KICKER/PUNTER MANUAL

Try-outs—no woulda, shoulda, coulda.

With my godson, M.

At a wedding with my cousin Brian.

Striking a pose in an alley.

Playing around on the computer.

Dad and Joshua.

Coach Clauer.

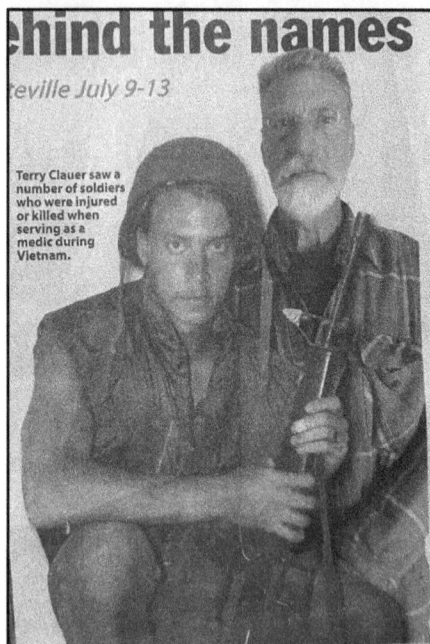
ehind the names

teville July 9-13

Terry Clauer saw a
number of soldiers
who were injured
or killed when
serving as a
medic during
Vietnam.

Dad's Vietnam story.

Working with boys like JA—
Joshua keeps his promises.

With baby Joshlynn after heart surgery.

Joshlynn up close.

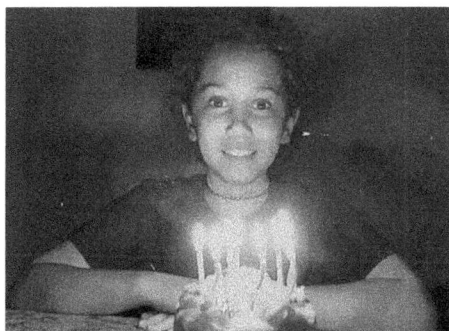

Joshlynn's birthday.

Joshlynn—practicin'.

Joshlynn and Joshua, teasing.

Grandpaw William Clauer, Joshua's namesake, about age 7.

Maw, Judith, Linda, Dad, and Kira, making book decisions, November 2021.

The Southside Raiders.

Mateo practicing.

Joshua and Mateo

All-American Division 3—Coaching the college special team.

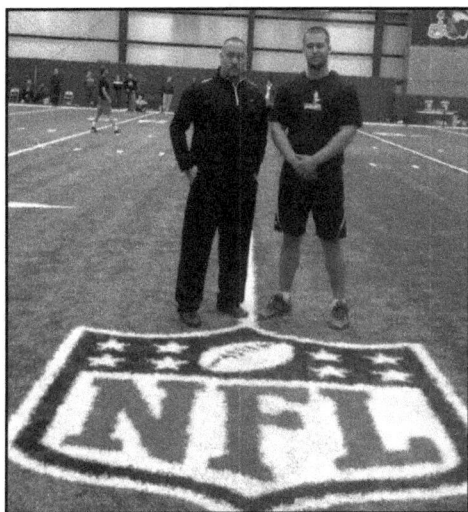

Coaching at football camp at the Minnesota Vikings' training camp.

173

Maw with football.

Maw and Joshua, November 2021.

A Sampling of Paintings by DarRen Morris

"On the inside looking out."

"Animal in a cage."

"Go Bears!" (Joshua and a young friend, initially painted for the cover of this book.)

"Soon to be Available."

"Caged."

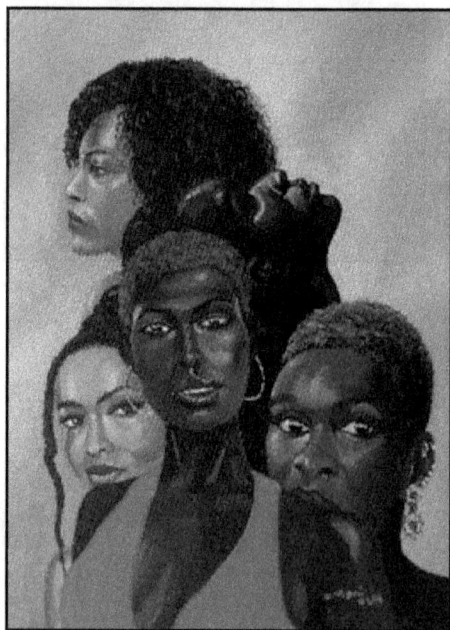

"Pillar of Strength."

ABOUT THE AUTHOR(S) AND THE ARTIST

Joshua William Clauer, the punter, has worked as a prison guard, a parole officer, and with returning prisoners through Madison Area Urban Ministry (dba Just Dane). He ultimately found his calling in working with pre-teen (mostly African American) boys helping them avoid gang involvement. Football has been one of the keys to helping his boys overcome the challenges they too often face. Born as "the boy with a bad heart," Joshua has surmounted his own obstacles as well. He knows the pathways.

Judith Gwinn Adrian, co-author. Joshua and Judy became a team, organizing and writing his memoir, mostly via Zoom meetings, during Covid-19. In recent years, Judy has written and/or co-written eight books (including *In Warm Blood: Prison and Privilege, Hurt and Heart*, with the artist who created the Bears' image in this book). Each of the books has been its own adventure. More detailed information at can be found at judithadrian.com.

The Bears' image painting is by DarRen Morris, a former street hustler and gang member from southern Wisconsin and northern Illinois, currently incarcerated. DarRen is self-taught, which means his art is not restricted to one style or medium. His work can be seen at darrenmorrisart.com.

www.ingramcontent.com/pod-product-compliance
Lightning Source LLC
Chambersburg PA
CBHW071338090426
42738CB00012B/2932